OUTSTANDING PRAISE FOR
VISIONS OF WAR, DREAMS OF PEACE

"OVERWHELMINGLY POWERFUL, SOUL-SEARING, AND PAINFULLY BEAUTIFUL. The poems express for many of us the feelings, thoughts and experience that was Vietnam."
—Rear Admiral Frances Shea Buckley

"WONDERFULLY RICH AND HAUNTING, A SEARING EVOCATION OF THE THRALL OF WAR."
—Bernard Edelman,
    editor of *Dear America: Letters Home from Vietnam*

"OFFERS US THE IMPORTANT AND OVERLOOKED PERSPECTIVES OF THE WOMEN WHO SERVED IN VIETNAM. We can honor their sacrifices and their courage by preserving and cherishing their insights. I believe that we owe them our attention and respect."
—United States Senator Daniel K. Inouye

ALSO BY LYNDA VAN DEVANTER

Home Before Morning

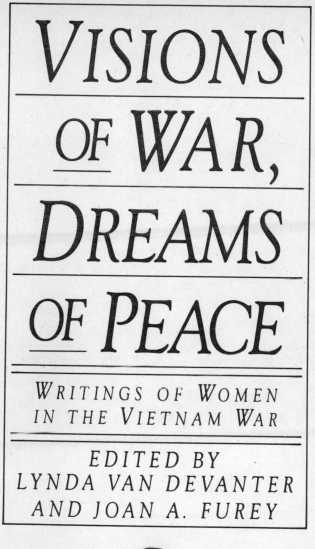

VISIONS
OF WAR,
DREAMS
OF PEACE

WRITINGS OF WOMEN
IN THE VIETNAM WAR

EDITED BY
LYNDA VAN DEVANTER
AND JOAN A. FUREY

WARNER BOOKS

A Time Warner Company

Royalties from the sale of this book are being donated by the authors to the Vietnam Women's Memorial Project, Inc. For further information about this organization, readers can contact the VWMP at 2001 "S" Street NW, Suite 302, Washington, DC, 20009. The VWMP is not responsible for the contents of this book and had no role in its creation.

Warner Books, Inc., 666 Fifth Avenue, New York, NY 10103

W A Time Warner Inc. Company

Printed in the United States of America
First printing: May 1991
10 9 8 7 6 5 4 3 2 1

Library of Congress Cataloging-in-Publication Data

Visions of war, dreams of peace : writings of women in the Vietnam War /
    edited by Lynda Van Devanter and Joan A. Furey.
    p.   cm.
    ISBN 0-446-39251-0
    1. Vietnamese Conflict, 1961–1975—Poetry.   2. Women soldiers-
-United States—Poetry.   3. American poetry—Women authors.
4. American poetry—20th century.   5. Soldiers' writings, American.
6. War poetry, American.   7. Peace—Poetry.   I. Van Devanter,
Lynda.   II. Furey, Joan A.
PS595.V5V57   1991
811'.54080358'082—dc20   90-23284
                                                              CIP

Cover design by Karen Katz
Cover photo by Sara McVicker
Book design by Giorgetta Bell McRee

To John and Juanita Furey
Who were always there for me
I miss you.

and

To Molly Eileen Buckley
With the fervent prayer that she never
has to learn first hand
what Mom did in the war.

ACKNOWLEDGMENTS

The putting together of a book of poetry by the women who served in Vietnam has been a dream of ours for over ten years. To finally see it happen is an experience that defies description. It would not have happened without the encouragement of our friends and colleagues who saw the value of the works included in this anthology and reinforced for us the importance of their message. To them we owe a great debt. Thanks to all of you.

A special thanks to Tom Buckley, Molly and Bridgid Buckley, Helen and Rodney Van Devanter, Mary Furey, Theresa Strynkowski, Vicki Staciwo, and Jack Furey, not only for their encouragement in this project, but for their love and support over the years. Thanks also to Joy Joffe, without whom some of these works would never have seen the light of day, and to Diane Carlson Evans, of the Vietnam Women's Memorial Project, our friend in Vietnam and our friend today, whose vision and tenacity has made the dream of a memorial to these women a reality.

We are grateful to Susan Suffes, our editor, who believed in this project from the start, and made our dream come true; to John Catterson, Bernie Edelman, Bill Ehrhart, Bruce Weigl, Gloria Emerson, Wayne Smith and Lady Borton, for their advice and guidance along the way; and to the William Joiner Center for the Study of War and Social Consequences at the University of Massachusetts, for providing us with a forum to exchange ideas and stimulate thinking.

Finally, we wish to thank the individual women whose works appear in this book, for their courage in sharing their most intimate of writings with us, and the many men and women veterans whom we have met over the years, who have shared with us their experience, strength, and hope. It is because of them that this book exists.

CONTENTS

RECOLLECTIONS

REFLECTIONS

AWAKENING

HEALING

LESSONS

DREAMS

FOREWORD

This book has been aching to come into being for a very long time. In 1972, when the remarkable and seminal anthology *Winning Hearts and Minds: War Poems by Vietnam Veterans* was published, it contained only two poems by women, only one of whom had actually been in Vietnam. In 1976, when the companion anthology *Demilitarized Zones: Veterans After Vietnam* was published, it contained only five poems by women, none of whom had been in Vietnam. In 1985, when *Carrying the Darkness: The Poetry of the Vietnam War* was published, it contained, again, only five poems by women, and, again, none of them had been in Vietnam.

Indeed, the very phrase "woman veteran," in the popular consciousness, seems almost a contradiction in terms. War is the domain of men. Women have no place in war. One measure of the depth of those perceptions—misperceptions, really—is that the U.S. government cannot even state with accuracy how many women served in Vietnam. To my great embarrassment, another measure is reflected in a poem I wrote about Vietnam veterans in 1972, which concludes: "We are your sons, America,/and you cannot change that./When you awake,/we will still be here." That the government can be so ignorant somehow does not surprise me, but that I could be so ignorant is a source of shame and embarrassment. I have often wondered, with no small discomfort, how women veterans feel when they read my poem.

For women did serve in Vietnam—as military nurses, logistical support personnel, USO staffers, Red Cross volunteers, and workers for a variety of private organizations like American Friends Service Committee and International Voluntary Services—an estimated 15,000 women, just as women have served in every U.S. war. Yet their sacrifices and suffering have been largely ignored, and they have been forced to bear a burden of silence even male veterans of Vietnam have not known, and indeed, wittingly and unwittingly, have even helped to foster, as my own insensitive words from "A Relative Thing" so bluntly confirm.

If male Vietnam veterans were met with indifferent silence when we came home, and for many years we were, we began to struggle against that silence almost immediately. War literature has a long tradition stretching back to *The Iliad* and beyond. And if what has been written by many men about Vietnam departs from that long tradition in refusing to romanticize or glorify war, still the tradition of male writing on war existed and needed only to be adapted to the situation. Thus, an enormous and still growing body of literature has come out of the Vietnam War, but if the amount of writing is astounding, the fact of it is not. Men wage war; men write about war.

No such tradition exists for women. Because they have been excluded from war in our cultural imagination, they have also been excluded from war literature. In the case of the Vietnam War, amid the hundreds and hundreds of books by men, there is only Gloria Emerson's *Winners and Losers*, Frances Fitzgerald's *Fire in the Lake*, Lynda Van Devanter's *Home Before Morning*, Lady Borton's *Sensing the Enemy*, Wendy Larson and Tran Thi Nga's *Shallow Graves*, and a small handful of others, almost none of which has been treated seriously by the popular, literary, scholarly, or historical communities.

I came to understand this terrible disparity only slowly and by fits and starts, but by the early 1980s, I at least knew it existed.

In 1984, when I was reading some 5,000 poems for possible inclusion in *Carrying the Darkness*, still not fully cognizant of the particular burden of silence borne by women veterans, I tried hard to locate poetry by women who had been in Vietnam. Nothing surfaced, but the nagging feeling persisted that it must be out there somewhere.

Then in 1987, at the Steinman Arts Festival at St. Lawrence University, I heard Norma Griffiths read some of her poems. She told the audience that she had begun writing as part of a therapy group in the early 1980s, and that she had never before shared any of her poems outside that group. Seventeen months later, I heard Marilyn McMahon read at the William Joiner Center for the Study of War and Social Consequences, University of Massachusetts at Boston. A year later, in the summer of 1988, Julia Perez, then director of the Joiner Center's Women Veterans Project, showed me a thick sheaf of poems by women veterans that she and Peggy Perri had been collecting. So it was there after all, untapped, unpublished, a lesson waiting to be taught, voices waiting to be heard.

When Lynda Van Devanter first told me about this book in July 1990, just about the first thing I said to her was: "I wanted these poems. I tried to find them for *Carrying the Darkness*. Why didn't anyone send me anything?"

"Of course, they wouldn't send you their poems," she replied. "You're a man."

"But I'm not that sort of a man," I protested, wounded by her reply.

"Yes, but they don't know that."

What they know is that I wrote a poem in 1972 that referred to Vietnam veterans as America's sons, that I published that poem in 1975 and many times thereafter, that not until 1989 did it finally appear in print with even a footnote acknowledging the grievous error contained therein. What they know is that the U.S. government, to this day, can't even say how many of them actually served in Vietnam. What they know is that the Vietnam Women's Memorial Project has met stiff resistance from people— men—who keep insisting that The Wall and the three male figures cast in bronze beside it is recognition enough for women.

Small wonder that these women wouldn't send me their poems. Thank God or whatever you believe in that they've been willing to send them to Lynda Van Devanter and Joan Furey—no small act of courage, that, given what they've had to live with all these years. And thanks to Van Devanter and Furey for having the courage, the vision, and the tenacity to see this dream into substance. These are voices that need to be heard. They are voices we need to hear. The experience of Vietnam in particular and war in general cannot be complete without them. And perhaps they will encourage other women veterans to write, and to share what they have written. Perhaps they may even help to drive home the reality that war and war literature belong not only to men, but to all humanity, and that the terrible cost of war has become too expensive to bear.

W. D. Ehrhart
Philadelphia, Pennsylvania
October 12, 1990

PREFACE

She said she had seen Hell and because she had seen Hell, she was set apart. Between her and every normal human pleasure, every normal human enjoyment, must stand the wards of Scutari. She could never forget. She wrote the words again and again in private notes, on the margins of letters, on scraps of blotting paper; whenever her hand lay idle, the phrase formed itself—"I can never forget."

If there is any reality about women and war it is embodied in the life of Florence Nightingale, about whom those words were written. If there is any myth of women and war it is probably most evident in the words of a New York publishing house editor who said in 1979, "What could a woman possibly have to say about war, especially the Vietnam War?"

For centuries women have gone to war. Frequently they have disguised themselves as men, often not had their true identities known. If thought of at all, they were usually thought of as saints or as sinners. And, almost always, they have been dismissed as unimportant after the war is over.

Men have written lyrically and gloriously about war after most conflicts. They have been published and written about, reviewed and discussed. They have been criticized, proclaimed, and exploited. They have had films and plays produced about their experiences. They have done books of fiction and nonfiction, prose and poetry. They *know* what war is.

Women, on the other hand, have come home from war and kept quite silent. They have gone back to their "duties," left the writing to the men. The number of "great books" about war by women can probably be counted on both hands. What they have written has not often described war as lyrical or glorious. What they have written has not often been reviewed or discussed, perhaps because it was not deemed important enough. Frequently it has been left off the lists and bibliographies of war literature. It has sometimes been filed under biography rather than war in libraries and bookstores. Few plays and films have been produced about women and their experiences. There is almost no published poetry by women about their wars.

With the publication of this book we hope to shatter one element of this myth. Women may have come home and gone back to their duties. They may have kept quiet. They may have left the publishing to men. But their experiences in war irrevocably changed them. They can never forget. They have felt the impact of war. They have written about it. The stories and books, the poems, plays, and songs have been written, make no mistake. But their writings have rarely seen the light of day. Usually they lie resting in an old shoe box, in the bottom drawer of the basement desk, on the highest shelf of the bookcase, or tucked away in the farthest reaches of the dresser drawer.

This book is the earliest venturing out of some of those hidden writings. The women whose poems are included here are absolutely courageous in their sharing of their innermost thoughts, feelings, pain, and growth; before, during, and after the Vietnam War. Very quietly, but nonetheless very distinctly, these women require that we hear and understand that they had a life-altering experience in Vietnam, and it is every bit as significant and important and definitive as anything that has been written by men about the war.

When men write about war, the themes often focus on the ambiguity of young males being handed power, frequently in the form of a gun, for the first time. They may describe the dark side of war, but usually balance that with the heroic, noble, and sometimes nostalgic. The writings of these women is less ambiguous. It is more about the consequences of war, consequences which these women have seen in a manner more harsh than most could imagine.

It has been said that the strength of writing is that in the specific is the universal. If that is true, then there are many universal truths in this volume. Some of the works contained in this anthology may not be what is referred to as great literature, but first writings rarely are. We believe the poems and thoughts in this book have great value beyond their literary quality. They help people to understand the reality of war from a perspective rarely seen or acknowledged. We hope that the reception given these works will encourage more women to write and publish, be reviewed, criticized, and proclaimed. These women need to be heard.

They *know* what war is.

Lynda Van Devanter Buckley
Joan A. Furey

When the power of love
Overcomes the love of power,
Then, and only then,
Shall we have peace.

Anonymous

Taken from a bulletin board
in the DaNang Red Cross Center,
Freedom Hill 1971

I
VISIONS

"I will never forget Vietnam . . . It is always there, and until the day that I am six feet under, Vietnam will always be there: the sights, the sounds, the smells, the happy times and the bad times . . . It is as real now as it was when I was there."

Maureen Nerli, USO
Tan Son Nhut, Vietnam
1985

"The aircraft was called a 'dust-off' . . . It was an ordinary thing for a reporter to do, riding choppers collecting the wrecked. One American, named John, was picked up for a head wound and lay on the floor, not dead or not alive. The medic could not stop the bleeding. There were never doors on the helicopters, so the wind moved his hair where the blood did not make it stick. It all becomes normal, the other correspondents, men, would say. In time, you'll see. They lied."

Gloria Emerson, Journalist
Vietnam
1972

DRIED CORSAGES

Dried corsages
tissue-shrouded
the last thing laid
into the crate

atop the diaries
atop the poems
atop the yearbooks
the detritus of adolescence.

The lid clicks
coffinlike
embalming my youth
in melancholy anticipation.

Last day of leave
last day of girlhood
last day of certitude
last day of luxuriant revokable errors.

First plane ride
first farewell
first overseas tour
first peek into womanhood's abyss.

The crumpled duffel awaits
decisions I can't make.
What do you pack
to take to a war?

Dana Shuster
1966

— *3* —

OKINAWA 1968

Dipping our words in white wine
we talk till morning, women
turning over moments
in rooms of coral and wind
because we do not know where we are.

The days on Okinawa are alike;
footprints down beach paths
from the beds we have left
at night the stars lick darkness.

The poinsettia is with us,
for a month the white lilies bloom
their fragrance like heavy cocoons
we wrap up in each time a touch

takes us close to the window where
we look at death there on the runway
fondling cities, suburbs, river valleys,
coordinates on maps, powers the fathers must

possess. To write it, to name it, to recover
our young selves, fading from the horizon
of history, our bodies, accidents on their runways.
Balconies of bombers overlook the rest of our lives.

Mary Pat O'Connor
1984

7 TIMES 52

Monday was a pink-orange malaria pill.
Tuesdaywednesdaythursdayfridaysaturdaysunday was one day.
Monday was a pink-orange malaria pill.
One communion replacing another.

Sharon Grant
1982

VIETNAM 1965

A sea of olive green
Covering the floor
Hanging from the rafters,
Sitting on the hill outside.

110 degrees radiating from
The roof of the very steel,
Very grey, very hot hangar.

Mildewed costumes that
Never dry
Blue clothed wounded in
Bandages with faces that
Match the color of the hangar.

Steel mesh screens across
The windows of our bus
Rifled guards outside our
Doors and windows.

Small arms fire in the distant hills
Seems like the 4th of July from our roof.
Fireworks, only for entertainment

Stomach cramps
Vomiting
Weakness
The food and water are not
From Oklahoma.

This market gives forth a
Sickening stench
Unlike Sears.
Women and babies
Babies and women
Five year old hustlers with
Candy bars and shoe polish.
Home is six inches on the curb

Judith Drake
1965

SAIGON

For Rudy Tram Van Phan

I can feel breezes fetid with *nuoc mam*,
I am drowned in vibrations of hondas.
My eyes scan horizons edged in bunkers
Framed by barbed wire.
I walk back streets lined by Ginkos,
Past French villas now stripped.
My eyes close in the wind and imagine
The time she was the Oriental Pearl.

Kathleen Trew
1970

FLASHBACK

Sky-blue Friday.
Behind the white buildings
the South China Sea.
Rows of silver pentagons flash on water
lazy breakers take gray waves.

If this is a war,
why am I swaying in a hammock
painting my nails coral,
planning a tan?

Sharon Grant
1982

IN THIS LAND

In this land of lush jungle and squalid
refugee camps, the beach and the patio form
a haven. A beach for play: smooth sand,
gentle waves. The patio for sitting, talking,
drinking: grey concrete, kept clean by mama-
sans with hose and broom; dotted with small
tables, each with its brightly striped umbrella.

She sits in a lawn chair, aluminum with yellow
webbing, exactly like those in Mom's backyard.
He sits in another, green.

The tropical sun is warm, quiet, serene.

Last night's explosions are over—forgotten—
as a bad dream is forgotten in the morning.
The breeze from the north is cooling, salt
laden as it moves from the Pacific across
the harbor to where they sit.

The noises of war: helicopters, jets, boat
engines; tanks, APC's, jeeps, Hondas are
ignored. Not heard. Only his deep voice,
sharing items of interest to colonels, and
her soft voice, responding to his rank and
masculinity. Her dress is sleeveless, short,
sunflower yellow, allowing her to bask in
the sun. It is not important that her role
is that of listener—admirer—the assigned
role of her sex for hundreds of years. It
is only important to feel warm, treasured,
wanted; safe for the moment. She squints

her eyes, idly scans the sun-glittered waves,
sips her gin and tonic, and listens with the
part of her brain not otherwise engaged.

He speaks of his days: how it is to be a
lawyer in a war zone, of a problem the Marines
are having with the Army. He speaks of
helicopter crashes, and botched rescues,
and negligence. She listens and nods, sunbathes
and daydreams. She gazes at the water, today
so similar to her own beloved Pacific, thousands
of miles away.

She notes that something new has appeared
on the waves. Idly she wonders that she had
not seen it before. She considers where it
might have come from and what it might be.
She watches, and sunbathes.

Her stomach begins to chill. She knows.
She asks: look, what is it? She is afraid
to say what she knows.

He cannot see it—continues to speak of what
is important to him. She is silent. The sun
glares, no longer warms. The ocean is foreign,
alien, violent. The object—she cannot
say its name yet—floats closer on the tide.

Finally others see it—but now there are
two—they launch a boat, row out to retrieve
the body. Another body. A third.
In flight suits, swollen with three days
submersion. White. Blue. Black. Khaki.

She remains silent. Ice cold. Unable to
see the white of the sun or the blue of the
waves, only the black of the shadows.

He becomes still.

The beach remains, sun-drenched, wave-washed.
The patio is clean, flat. Empty.

Marilyn McMahon
1988

A BOOM, A BILLOW

While waiting for a plane to DaNang
I watched American bombers a mile away.
The uninvolved objectivity with which I stared at the sleek
    jets,
their wings sloping back in fiercely powerful lines,
confused and disturbed me.
The jets swooped down,
then up quickly,
to circle and swoop once more.
A boom.
A billow of dark gray smoke.
Napalm.

That afternoon I met a boy at the Helgoland hospital ship.
He sought me out because I came from Quang Ngai,
his ancestral home.
He had no nose,
only two holes in the middle of his face.
His mouth was off to the side.
One eye was gone;
there was a hollow in his forehead above the other.
All his face was shiny red scar tissue.
Most of the rest of his body was the same.
One hand was partly usable,
the fingers of the other,
soldered to his wrist.
Napalm.

Lady Borton
1972

THE BEST ACT IN PLEIKU,
NO ONE UNDER 18 ADMITTED

I kissed a Negro, trying to breath life into him.
When I was a child—back in the world—
the drinking fountains said, "White Only."
His cold mouth tasted of dirt and marijuana.
He died and I put away the things of a child.

Once upon a time there was a handsome, blond soldier.
I grabbed at flesh
combing out bits of shrapnel and bits of bone
with bare fingers.

A virgin undressed men,
touched them in public.
By the time I bedded a man
who didn't smell like mud and burned flesh
He made love and I made jokes.

Sharon Grant
1982

KENNY

while i was out building morale
you
with your Cobra
were dying.

details are relative,
your wife waits
unknowing that i think of her at this moment
or
that you never again will.

last night you were drunk
and we wanted to be alone
so we made excuses
and left you

i'm sorry now
but it's much too late for apologies
you're too busy derosing from the world
and being reassigned to eternity
to know how i feel.

dwelling upon the loss of a friend
is death in life

life is for the living
death is for the dead
and so Kenny,
we must now go our separate ways.

the sad part
is not that you're dead.
the sad part is
that you are no longer alive.

i'll miss you.

emily strange
1969

LIKE SWANS ON STILL WATER

Like swans on still water they skim over the war
Ao dais gliding, rustling serenely
gleaming black hair pulled primly away
from faces that reveal nothing save inner repose,
a beauty so deep even war can't defile.

I note my reflection in their obsidian eyes—
an outsized barbarian, ungainly, unkempt,
baggy in ever-wilted greens,
five-pound boots taking plowhand strides,
face perpetually ruddy, dripping in alien heat.

In their delicate presence I exhume teenage failures—
the girl in the back row forever unnoticed,
the one no one ever invited to dance,
the one never voted most-likely anything,
the one who was never quite something enough.

But once in a while, on a crazy-shift morning,
when I've worked through the night and I'm too tired to care,
a young man who reeks of rice paddies lies waiting
for someone to heal the new hole in his life.
He says through his pain, all adolescent bravado,
"Hey, what's your name? Let's get married. I love you."

And just for a moment I become Nefertiti
and for all the Orient's pearls and silks
I would not trade the glamour and privilege
of these honored hands, licensed to touch
one filthy GI.

Dana Shuster
1966

HOW DO YOU SAY I LOVE YOU IN A WAR?

I

I couldn't believe what I was seeing.
All the GIs kept telling me that these people
aren't like us.
They don't value life as we do.
How then do you explain that woman when told her son was
    dead,
how do you explain her beating her head
against the pavement until her blood flowed
and mingled with his?

II

I was brought up to think of prostitutes
as something outside myself.
It never occurred to me to feel sorry for them.
Why then would Sno spend all the money
she earned last week,
to buy me a present?

III

Little war baby, so helpless, so sick, so weak.
They tell me you can't make it
until the next supply shipment arrives
and I can't come back this way.
I would give you the food from my mouth.
It is one thing to help a grown man die,
it is quite another not to be able
to help a baby live!

What can I do for you?
I hold you and that says I love you,
I clean your festered skin and that says I love you
But nothing I can do is enough.
I shall remember you all my life.
I shall remember you most when I hold my own.
If I love him, in remembrance of you,
perhaps that will be enough.

IV

Sometimes when it hurt too much
or when the guilt piled up
or the loneliness became overwhelming
some of the guys would play
long, haunting melodies on the sour old guitars
warped from the constant wetness.
Inevitably there would be a Baptist among us
usually a black, black lad from Georgia or Alabama
whose velvet, wordless voice would make us weep
I tried not to
for fear it would never stop.

V

It's only a telegram,
typed out words, common words, you use every day,
words that usually mean nothing.
How could that young wife know how my heart broke?
How could she know how much I loved her
when I stood over her young,
battered and broken lieutenant
and wrote those stupid, stupid words?
"Honey, I love you. Don't worry about me."
How can she ever forgive me?

VI

I stare and wonder at you
and you at me
and we are enemies.
You killed my brother. He shot you.
You left your rice paddy for the enemy's hospital.
I left my cornfield for my brothers
in that hospital.
I should hate you. You should hate me.
Why do we stare?
You take hold of my hand and love passes
through our fingers.
Who is our enemy, if we love one another?

Bobbie Trotter
1981

VO THI TRUONG

My day starts when I see Truong.
She lives in the hospital's paraplegic ward
where her mother has been a patient for over a year.
Truong's mother suffers from the results of a bullet
that damaged her spinal cord
while she was planting rice.
She will live another month,
perhaps.

There is no full-time medical care on this ward.
A few nurses dispense pills and dress bedsores,
but there is no staff to turn patients,
much less bathe them.
Most patients have a family member to nurse them.
This is Truong's job.
She is three years old.

Every day Truong,
dangling an intravenous bottle behind her,
wanders out to the food stalls near the hospital gate
to buy tea for her mother.
Later she dumps a bottle filled with urine
onto the grass mat in front of the ward.
Emptying her mother's catheter
is another of Truong's chores.

Truong is supposed to wait for me in front of the paraplegic
    ward
for a ride to a nearby day-care center,
but she is seldom there.
I look around the ward.
And almost invariably I find her

peeping out from where she sleeps,
in the spilled urine under her mother's bed.
Her hands jump up to cover her mischievous grin.
She wriggles out,
runs over and hugs my legs,
giggling.
That is when my day begins.

Lady Borton
1972

MAMASAN

For Ms. Dung

Mamasan
Squats at her basin
Wringing out endless chatter
Through blackened teeth that hide her smile.
Waddling off,
Her sandals flap.
Orange clouds of dust
Chase black silk pajamas
That scurry in the breeze
To cover bowed legs.
She filters out of our world
Back to hers
Through a simple gate.

Kathleen Trew
1970

TWO VILLAGES

In Duc Ninh a village of 1,654 households
Over 100 tons of rice and cassava were burned
18,138 cubic meters of dike were destroyed
There were 1077 air attacks
There is a bomb crater that measures 150 feet across
It is 50 feet deep

Mr. Tat said: The land is more exhausted than the people
                I mean to say that the poor earth
                is tossed about
                thrown into the air again and again
                it knows no rest

                whereas the people have dug tunnels
                and trenches   they are able in this way
                to lead normal family lives

    In Trung Trach
 a village of 850 households
a chart is hung in the House of Tradition

rockets	522
attacks	1201
big bombs	6998
napalm	1383
time bombs	267
shells	12291
pellet bombs	2213

Mr. Tuong of the Fatherland Front
has a little book
in it he keeps the facts
carefully added

Grace Paley
1971

— 24 —

WALKING CLASS

Nguyet organized a walking class for amputees.
Their legs were in varying stages of development.
Some were still roughly hewn chunks of lumber,
others sculptured imitations of the good leg.
The patients struggled to activate these strange inert
    appendages.

Nguyet drew lines on the floor for a race.
Each person had to step on every line as he crossed the room.
The patients laughed at old Buoi
when he tried to sneak a head start
and cheerfully taunted Toi when she overstepped a line
and had to return to "Go."

A crowd of spectators cheered them on.
Double amputees and paraplegics
spun their wheelchairs around each other
for a better view.
A band of children not wearing legs
darted back and forth across the course,
on their crutches,
as they teased the contestants.

Lady Borton
1972

VIETNAM

V isions of justness;
I mpressions of horror;
E mptiness of soul;
T actics of dishonesty;
N aked of spirit;
A ction of politics;
M asters of denial.

Janet Krouse Wyatt
1986

SATURDAY NIGHT

Saturday night
Oldies night
on AFVN
Letter-writing night
Toenail-painting night
fantasy-spinning night

Watching the geckoes
dancing across the wall
like-poled magnets
maintaining measured distance
Buddy Holly and
bubble-gum rock
recall high school and home

Rainy season mildew
smells like Houston
Rain on the roof
at 80 drops per minute
like lactated Ringer's
clear and steady
unlike me

Silence shattered
by artillery boys
across the road
playing with guns
No dates tonight
for these teen warriors
firing H & I

"Harassment and Interdiction"—
harassing only my rest
interdicting only my dreams

I turn up the radio
and pray for peace

Dana Shuster
1967

HOLY SATURDAY 1971

On Holy Saturday all the church
Doors and windows stayed open.
Ed was my first lover.
When he made Aircraft Commander
I sent him a silver cup.

"We're sending you another patient.
Gunshot wound of the abdomen
Filthy dirty.
Watch his BP, he might still bleed out."
Red camellias bloomed outside the church.

"His name is Ed Welch."

Cold.
My hand hurts around the iron bed.
A bird flew in looking for the Holy Ghost.

Ed drank Black Russians.
His mustache tickled of kahlua and JP-4.
I would grip his damp curls.
Beside the tabernacle the silver cup
Stood empty.

The man they bring me is a sergeant
I have never seen him before.

The red candle wasn't lit.

Sharon Grant
1982

— 29 —

MELLOW ON MORPHINE

Mellow on morphine, he smiles and floats
above the stretcher over which I hover.
I snip an annular ligament
and his foot plops unnoticed into the pail,
superfluous as a placenta after labor has ended.
His day was just starting when his hootch disappeared,
along with the foot and at least one friend.
Absently I brush his face,
inspecting, investigating,
validating data gathered by sight and intuition,
willing physical contact to fetter soul to earth.

"You the first white woman ever touch me."

Too late my heart dodges and weaves, evades the inevitable.
Ambushed again.
Damn, I'm in love.
Bonded forever by professional intimacies,
unwitting disclosures offered and accepted,
fulfilling a covenant sealed in our chromosomes,
an encounter ephemeral as fireflies on a hot Georgia night
in a place and time too terrible to be real.
But it will shoot flaming tracers through all my dreams
until the time my soul, too, floats unfettered.

When daylight waxes and morphine wanes,
when pain crowds his brain
and phantasms of his footless future bleach the bones of
    present
our moment together will fade as a fever dream
misty, gossamer, melting from make-believe
through might-have-been

past probably-didn't
all the way into never happen, man—
as I move on to the next stretcher
and the next fleeting lover—
silken memories mounting, treasures in my soul.

Dana Shuster
1967

MY SON'S CHILDHOOD

What do you have for a childhood
That you still smile in the bomb shelter?
There is the morning wind which comes to visit you
There is the full moon which follows you
The long river, the immense sea, a round pond
The enemies' bomb smoke, the evening star.
At three months you turn your head, at seven you crawl
You toy with the earth, you play with a bomb shelter.
I long for peace every day, every month for a year
For a year, you toddle around the shelter.
The sky is blue, but way over there
The grass is green far away on the ancient tombs.
My heart is a pendulum
Pounding my chest, keeping time for the march.
The small cricket knows to dig a shelter
The crab doesn't sleep: it, too, fears the bombs.
In the moonlight, even the hare hides.
The black clouds hinder the enemy's sight.
Flowers and trees join the march
Concealing troops crossing streams, valleys, villages.
My son, trenches crisscross everywhere.
They're as long as the roads you'll someday take.
Our deep shelter is more precious than a house.
The gun is close by, the bullets ready
If I must shoot.
When you grow up, you'll hold life in your own hands.
Whatever I think at present
I note down to remind you of your childhood days.
In the future, when our dreams come true,
You'll love our history all the more.

Xuan Quynh
1969
(Translated by Phan Thanh Hao with Lady Borton)

THE KID

His was the smooth, soft skin
of light blond hair and ruddy cheeks.
Easy to embarrass. Shaved once
a week or less, never
flunked inspections.
A boy who volunteered,
didn't wait for the draft.
Called "kid" by everyone
in the platoon.

A week of patrols,
then his squad went to China Beach.
"Three beers, I swear to God,
ma'am, he only had three beers."
The sergeant was crying.
The kid had fallen. A simple fall.
A head injury. Brain stem damage.
Inoperable.
No hope.

Three days, he lay there. A machine
breathing for him. Nurses
and corpsmen bathing him, turning
him, protecting him from nighttime
rockets. He didn't need a shave.
Test after test, no change.
No chance. A simple fall.
No bullets, no mortars, no chance.
The fourth day,
I removed the respirator
and waited.
Hours later, his heart stopped.

Marilyn McMahon
1990

— 33 —

LETTER FROM HOME

Got a down-home letter from my momma today.

It came all the way from the big PX
on the peaceful side of the planet—
land of perfume
and powder puffs
and poodles on leashes.
It was written on petite pink paper
fenced round by thornless roses.

It was chock plumb full of down-home news.
Football pre-season practice started
And it's been hot and awful dry
And a jarhead name Whitman
wasted a dozen-odd students
from a window in the UT tower.

Momma doesn't know what this world's coming to.
But she says nobody I know got killed.
Momma is real glad I'm in Vietnam
working in a hospital where I am safe
where nobody I know gets killed.

Guess Cu Chi doesn't make Momma's down-home news.

Dana Shuster
1966

VIGIL

Legs ache, head throbs
Every muscle taut
Every nerve on edge
I want to scream but I can't

Day after day, week after week
A parade.
What about his family,
his girlfriend—his wife and kids.
He's maimed, stumps where once
there was a leg and arm. A face even
adults will hide from.

Their future?
Mustn't think of that.
It could tear you to pieces
giving them an identity
of more than SOLDIER?

He's one, look at them all
those who died, those who left,
blind, deformed, paralyzed.
Young men,
bright, handsome, funny.
Now sad and confused and wondering
Why me?

I don't know, I can't answer that.
I know it hurts, you have to expect some pain.
Why Nurse? Why me?

I wish I knew. Why you,
Why him, Why them, Why me.

And when I leave
What will I be?
I can't be what I was before
I can't be what I am during
I must be something else

I'm sorry, it got to me today
I'm a nurse and maybe it shouldn't.
but it does, And I ask also
Why God? Why?

Joan A. Furey
1969

SISTER MARY

Standing there in subdued light, bewildered.
So pale in her fatigues, the beads of sweat roll down her face,
as she contemplates how to do more.
Giving everything she has, wearily wondering
if this is what Sister Mary meant by
"offering it up"?

Each new broken being she tenderly enfolds
Within her nurturing eldest daughter heart
Caring without ceasing, praying for hope,
Yearning for strength and yet with shadows of guilt regretting
There's just not enough for them and her too
"Mea culpa"?

Oh, she would know then, and again and again and again
That somehow she "should have done more," but could she?
Yes, she learned well that each soul was as the broken body
of Sister Mary's Jesus.
But now could she see beyond the pain of all the unfulfilled
    dreams,
theirs, hers and Sister Mary's.
"Mea maxima culpa"?

Penny Kettlewell
1990

THE FRIENDSHIP
ONLY LASTED
A FEW SECONDS

He said "Mom,"
And I responded
And became her.
I never lied
to him.
And I couldn't
Explain that to others.
I got all and more back.
But the friendship
Only lasted a few seconds.

And he called me Mary.
I wished she could
Be there for him.
I felt I was in
Second place,
But I did the
Best I could
And the friendship
Only lasted a few seconds.

And he told me,
"I don't believe this,
I'm dying for nothing."
Then he died.
Again, the friendship
Only lasted a few seconds.

How can the World
Understand any of this?
How can I keep the
World from forgetting?
After all the friendship
Only lasted a few seconds.

Lily Lee Adams
1981

DEAR MOM

Now please don't panic,
but just in case,
there are some things I should tell you.

I guess it's pride in our own individuality,
or self-doubt of our own womanhood
that makes it hard for mothers and daughters to talk.
There's a great mystery to being a woman,
a greater mystery, I now know,
to being a mother.

Mothers are so close to life.
I must share with you,
I have been here almost a year now,
and so far as I know,
every man who has died,
had the same last word on his lips—
"Mother"

Bobbie Trotter
1981

THE VIETNAMESE MOTHER

One night in late 1965
A Vietnamese mother received a letter
From her beloved child
In the battlefield
Telling her of his first memories of war.
He'd seen a young American soldier
Agonizing
As he let out his last sigh.
"Oh Mama!" the American had cried.
Tears filled the Vietnamese mother's eyes.

Seven years later
Waiting for her son's letter
Her hair now white
When a letter finally arrived. But
Not his handwriting this time.
Strange feelings
Her heart tightens
A friend of his writes
"Oh Mama!" he cried before he died
Bathed in moonlight.

Day after day
She reads the few letters since 1965
Again and again she cries
For her lost son
And for an unknown American mother
Who lost her beloved child.

Huong Tram
1976
(Translated by Phan Thanh Hao
with Lady Borton)

PRE-OP

For Marie

A doorgunner lay on a litter,
Rigid, immobile
In the shock-ice
Of fear and pain
Into twilight sleep
Falling.
Never to see the care in her smile
Or hear the sanity in her jokes.
Falling,
Never to feel the touch
That wiped Asian dust from his forehead.

Kathleen Trew
1970

HELLO, DAVID

Hello, David—my name is Dusty.
I'm your night nurse.
I will stay with you.
I will check your vitals
   every 15 minutes.
I will document
   inevitability.
I will hang more blood
   and give you something
   for your pain.
I will stay with you
   and I will touch your face.

Yes, of course,
   I will write your mother
   and tell her you were brave.
I will write your mother
   and tell her how much you loved her.
I will write your mother
   and tell her to give your bratty kid sister
   a big kiss and hug.
What I will not tell her
   is that you were wasted.

I will stay with you
   and I will hold your hand.
I will stay with you
   and watch your life
   flow through my fingers
   into my soul.
I will stay with you
   until you stay with me.

Goodbye, David—my name is Dusty.
I am the last person
   you will see.
I am the last person
   you will touch.
I am the last person
   who will love you.

So long, David—my name is Dusty.
David—who will give me something
   for my pain?

Dusty
1986

CHEATED

She tells me I have been cheated
Because I didn't know you
Perhaps not
I knew you better than most.

It was your arm, leg, lung, brain, heart
I knew most intimately
I didn't know your identity
But it was better for me.

Names, hometowns that might be
Too close to my own
I would then have to think of you
As a person
Better just a body
It was better for me.

I can survive this nightmare
This very long year
By not knowing you
Not knowing where you are from
Just flesh
Not a real person
It is better for me.

I want to follow you
From the OR to the ward
Did you make it home OK?
Did you survive?
Who are you?

I must not allow myself
To get too close
The distance
Is better for me.

Mary Lu Ostergren Brunner
1984

THE COFFEE ROOM SOLDIER

I walked into the coffee room for a cup of brew.
The push was over and I needed energy to re-group
for the next assault on our forces
and on my senses.

I initially stepped casually over his shattered body
laid out, unbagged, on the coffee room floor
out of the way
thinking, where would I find them next:
in my bed?

I turned with cup in hand and ascertained the damage.
His chest wall blown away, exposing his internal organs
An anatomical drawing.
Dispassionately I assessed his wounds
and sipped from my cup.

I then saw his face
that of a child in terror
and only hours ago
alive as I
or maybe I was dead as he,
because with another sip, a cigarette and a detached analysis
I knew I could no longer even feel.

I stepped out and grabbed a mop and pail
so we would stop slipping in the blood on the R&E floor
bagged the extra body pieces and the coffee room soldier
re-stocked supplies, then went outside to watch the sunrise,
alone and destitute of tears.

Penny Kettlewell
1990

I KNOW YOU'VE WAITED

I know you've waited
A long, hard time for me
And yes, I am coming home.
But in all fairness,
I am not the same person you loved then.
We'll need time.

Bobbie Trotter
1981

II
RECOLLECTIONS

"I remember how they came in all torn up. It was incredible. The first time a medevac came in. I got right into it. I didn't have a lot of feeling at that time. It was later on that I began to have a lot of feeling about it, after I'd seen it over and over and over again."

Gayle Smith, Army Nurse
Binh Thuy, Vietnam
1981

THE TROUBLE IS TRITENESS

The trouble with attending a war is
One feels so guilty to come back alive.
Death and torn flesh one writes about is
Theirs. There are no adjectives to contrive
That are more red than blood, more quiet than
    death,
More stark than real, more sharp than pain,
More absent than gone, more still than breath
That can never be diaphragmed again.
So, trite as poems may be about a war,

There is one scene that says it all to me.
A child's hand lay, palm up, on a floor . . .
Beseeching, poignant, searing memory.
    Real action and hot lights, continuous text.
    Bandages and blood, continuous, next . . .
Next!

                                Winifred Schramm, Army Nurse
                                Anzio, WW II
                                1947

FLASHBACKS

Flashbacks,
Dreams,
Snatches,
of what I do not want
to recall . . . .

Norma J. Griffiths
1982

HOW MANY SOUNDS?

How many sounds make a memory?
Funny thing to think sitting on a porch in El Porto
Waiting for the dawn
But the sea sounds the same here as in Qui Nhon
And chimes still ring when a breeze catches them.

An occasional car passes madly by
4 AM brings out the madness in everything
No sounds of distant or near guns
They're replaced by the constant crackling of power lines
And I remember incessant hours listening to choppers
Wondering if the endless procession would ever stop.

No howling of sentry dogs breaks the stillness
Nor whoosh of flares to make day out of night
Instead, the refinery is burning off
Making it difficult to tell where man leaves off
and God's new born sun begins.

> Lynda Van Devanter Buckley
> *1972*

ROW UPON ENDLESS ROW

It was the summer of 1971
America seemed wild and frightening,
brazen with freeways.

Driving from Washington to Boston
I lost my way.
The July heat was heavy.

Passing buildings pulsed with neon.
Signs and exits raced by.
Trucks loomed up behind me
blowing their air horns.

Then,
on both sides of the highway,
as far as I could see,
stretched a graveyard.
Stone after gray stone.

Rain started to fall
Thunder shook the air
each crack like an exploding mortar.
Panic welled deep in my chest.

The tombstones went on and on
like rows of parading soldiers.
It rained harder,
and I turned up the radio.

The rain poured with the savagery of a monsoon
For a split second the wipers flicked the waves away
and once again I saw gravestones,
row upon endless row.

The radio announcer listed the body count
for American soldiers
disregarding the Vietnamese.

The tombstones and spires
and mausoleums darkened,
closing in.

The road and the water grayed
until panic washed over me.
I pulled off onto the shoulder of the road
and wept.

Lady Borton
1984

TO AN PHU

(*An Phu is a village in Cu Chi district, which is 40 miles from Ho Chi Minh City/Saigon. Cu Chi is famous for its tunnels.*)

I love this plot of land
not just like a first love
not just like love at first sight.

I come here—
the noon wind is mixed with sand
the heat glancing off a bomb crater dries my face
the bumpy field is covered with ash.

Here, there's no shadow from a single bird
no trace of calm countryside
no betel trees or stacks of straw
nor thresholds worn with the tread of generations
not even the voices of birds nesting at dusk.

On this land
horror roots in the mind
terrible memories become an imprisoned wound
that love can never parole.

I see flash images that remind me of my mother
my mother planting vegetables
my mother transplanting rice
my mother digging trenches
my mother carrying weapons
I miss my mother
when those images flash.

I love this place
I love the climate
the perfume of the land
the wild grass
echoing
the rainy season's first thunder.

I love this place
I love its far-away wind
whispering in my ear like Grandmother's voice
    full of legends
the broad wind
the long wind
so immense
across a plain stripped of houses.

But the river still flows gently like a folk song
The tide runs out towards the city
I love this place where the water reflects the sun
Oh An Phu Village
how beautiful
is my love.

Ha Phuong, written in a Cu Chi tunnel,
1974
(Translated by Phan Thanh Hao
with Lady Borton)

RECOLLECTION

I close my eyes and conjure up
visions of things past.

Unwillingly, unknowingly—like the
blinking of an eye, the twitch of a muscle.

Visions of men, young and old.
so many young and also old.

The gift of life slowly drips from its container
to form a puddle on the floor
beneath your head.

PUMP! PUMP! PUMP!
Try in vain to replace what is going
and gone.

Streaks of crimson in waves of gold
on sea of green and shore so white
so very white.

What purpose has brought you here?
to lie so still,
to think no thoughts,
to cease to dream and care and be.

The nature of your mission,
locked in your soul.
The reason for you living,
in another's heart.

The vision of your death,
in the folds of my mind.

Joan A. Furey
1970

A NURSE'S LAMENT

I saw the horror in the young man's eyes;
A fear of certain death.
I heard the cries of tortured souls;
Of dreams that once were real.

I touched the skin of a dead man's face;
A cold and unforgiving end.
I smelled the blood and filth;
Of men that once were boys.

I tasted gall as the tragedy grew;
A senseless war, at best
I thought I knew what lay ahead;
But that was purely in my mind.

Janet Krouse Wyatt
1987

DREAMS THAT BLISTER SLEEP

You try to repress them because you know.
In scraps of sleep you want another chance.
You are probably going to come back.

You strip-searched the mama-sans for the man.
You didn't know about sisterhood then. Now
You try and repress them because you know.

You piece shards of friendship to keep Barry
Alive. You saw him his last day. You owe him.
You are probably going to come back.

Sudden gunfire in a play. You can't stop
Crying. The tears break you ten years late.
You try and repress them because you know.

You take your man's abuse for years. He leaves.
Did Vietnam cripple you or him? You know
You are probably going to come back.

Dreaming the guts out of faded pictures,
Scratchy tapes, a diary. Devouring them
You try and repress them because you know
You are probably going to come back.

                                    Sharon Grant
                                    1982

SAVING LIVES

How old were you then—17?—18?—and I, 22?

The platoon was to call you "Doc"
And you would bandage, splint and tourniquet
Give the morphine, save their lives.

They'd need you when the shrapnel flew
Rounds that enlarge after entering flesh,
Missiles, mines, grenades.

Blood, burns, needles, dressings, charts,
Swiftly you learned in months
What cost me college years.

We became akin in helping others
My corpsmen, partners, friends.

The orders came and off you went
The party, good-bye, God Bless.

A new group would arrive
And we'd begin again.

Yesterday, I went to the "Wall"
Dear God—
I found you there!

Mary O'Brien Tyrrell
1986

ROAD SHOW

For Greg

I walked around my feelings then
On endless detour
Never time to fix my eyes into yours.
I worked twelve-hour shifts
For an Asian carnival.
I was filled with unquenchable thirst
For frolic
For idle conversation.
You tried to catch me but I couldn't stop my carousel.
You worked twelve hours too,
Fixing heads on broken puppet soldiers
Never needing the mask of a carnival clown.
Gypsy Prince
You knew time's passage would give direction to lone clowns
   walking.
You saw detours end on the highways paved
With feelings never merged
On eyes never focused
In rusted Asian carnivals.

                                        Kathleen Trew
                                        1970

ONE SMALL BOY

Darkness creeps slowly around me.
Thunderclouds roll in, filling the sky.
The heart bleeds when struck by metal.

A boy of eight, nine, maybe ten years
Lies on a gurney.
One single wound.
A red fountain arches to the sky
As I take away the cloth.

I can never forget
How I backed away
My tears falling on that small boy's face.
As Death came in
And took away
One small boy.

Twenty years
And still I feel the pain of my crime
The crime of being afraid,
Afraid of watching small boys pass away
Afraid of watching young men die.

Kathleen F. Harty
1990

RECOVERY

They didn't say much in recovery,
especially the head wounded.
Airway pulled, vital signs stable, heads raised,
ready to roll over to ward 5.
Some called it the vegetable patch.

Not forty-five minutes out of surgery,
head big with bandages
one side of his body paralyzed like an old man
this one was wide awake and flirting.
"Hey, you're cute," he said.

Surprised and flattered, I grinned wide
and wished I really was cute.
Twenty years later his next words still turn me cold.
"I was a steeplejack."

Mary Beyers Garrison
1990

VIETNAM, OPPRESSIVE HEAT

Vietnam, Oppressive Heat—
The Malignant Stench Compressing The Senselessness Of—
Dying Life And Living Death
Of Frenzy, Fear, Frustration—
Conceived By Doubt, Deceit And Damnation.
Wrought of Human Sacrifice—
Theirs And,
Ours—

Penny Kettlewell
1990

IN MEMORIUM

The ER was so busy with the wounded—so damn young—
    the cries and smells were background, the "push"
      had just begun.

The day comes back so clearly, death is vivid in
    my eye; a memory that comes haunting me these
      many years gone by. . . .

The back room called "Expectant," where those not
    yet gone would pass—where the hope for saving
      had been lost, and they would breathe their last.

I recall a young man—his hair was red—his name
    to me unknown; I sat with him and held his hand
      so he wouldn't die alone.

I cursed all wars, the useless waste, the loss
    and grief to all, and I asked WHY? it came to
      be we ever killed at all.

I waited at this young man's side, thought of
    family unaware that their loved one lies here
      dying, a life that wasn't spared.

I prayed for them and hoped that time would ease
    their grief, their pain; that as their lives
      continued on, they'd feel joy and smile again.

The time did come when this soldier died, and
    I stood up to leave, but I never left his memory
      there, and for his loss I grieve.

And as I stand before the Wall, these thoughts
    flash through my head, to that kid I knew of
      years ago, a kid that I called Red.

Joan Parrot Skiba
1987

THE TEARS

I don't remember
Ever discussing
The patients
After they left
R & E

Either walking
by litter
or bag . . . . .

Perhaps no one
wanted
to be the weakling
and show
publicly
the tears . . . . .

Norma J. Griffiths
1982

EYES

Eyes are the mirror of the soul,
A bodily organ projecting emotions
which can't be hidden.

My eyes are the only part of my face
which speaks to you
in the confusion of our surroundings.

You are watching my eyes
for some sign to assure you
that perhaps the blood you taste
and swallow until it chokes you,
is not your own.

You seek some assurance
that the burning pain of your seared flesh
will cease when you awake
from what you hope
is some demented joke or diabolical dream.

There is an immediate bond between us.
The lower half of my face is concealed
by a surgical mask.
The lower part of yours,
torn away by an act of war.

Your attempt to speak is futile,
terror strikes your eyes
as you begin to strangle.

Your hands gesture frantically
communicating your fear.

As you reach toward your face
my hands catch yours.

Our eyes lock,
I must decide if the reassurance you seek
should be the truth or
empty platitudes.

Certainly, it would be easier to say,
"Lay quiet, everything will be alright."
But my eyes would attest to the lie
and I feel you would live to hate me for it.

The truth is,
I have never seen a man
with the lower half of his face torn
brutally apart.

There is little remaining to identify you,
yet here you lie, awake and staring
at me.
Wanting an answer to the question:
"Please! How bad is it?"

My insides churn,
I'd like to turn and run,
bury my head in someone's shoulder,
scream, then cry.

Instead, I swallow hard,
wipe the blood from your eyes
and tell you the truth, pausing momentarily
to say we will try our very best.

You reach up and take the mask from my face.
A smile of encouragement and tear-filled eyes
greet you.
I am touched by the humanity
we share.

In the 13 hours that follow,
we try to reconstruct your face.
Are we playing God?

Later, your head a mass of bandages
and drainage tubes,
your eyes say it all.
"I made it!"

In the hours that follow
as sleep eludes me,
I wonder.
Will you live to curse us
for your life
or will your courage overcome
the obstacles ahead?

Years have passed
and I am seeing your eyes again.
I see the hope and courage I saw then
and silently pray
that this is true
rather than to think
your life became so unbearable,
your emotional pain so intense,
you chose an abrupt and brutal end.

I will take my mask off
if it will help
again.
But when I start to cry,
I am afraid
I won't be able to stop.

You see
I need to know that your wounds healed,
that you can smile again
and laugh.
Then I, too, will be at peace.

Helen DeCrane Roth
1990

III
REFLECTIONS

LEFT BEHIND

I search my soul
And memories of war
To find that lost space
That part of me that's gone
Left in Vietnam so many
Years ago and hoping
Someday to find it and
Make me whole again
I didn't leave behind
A limb, an arm or a leg
What is it then that's gone
It can't be seen and
Perhaps just as a lost
Limb it can never be
Retrieved

Diane Carlson Evans
1984

"Now, for me, the war is over and my Red Cross work
is finished. I cannot express the dreadful emptiness

which has come into my life. Anna Ivanova found me weeping one day; I could not tell her why, because I, myself did not know. She said it was "reaction." I did not contradict her, but I knew it was something much deeper than that. As I looked through these fragmentary notes of mine, I relived all the tragic scenes again and asked myself: 'Was it I, really I—who saw that? Was it I, really I—who did that?' From where had the strength come to endure those ghastly moments? I shivered at the memories they brought back. I recalled the desolate battlefields and saw the soldiers lying amid the twisted wires and shell cavities. Will they be remembered? But who could remember all those many thousands and thousands?"

Florence Farmborough, Red Cross Nurse
The Russian Front, WW I
1918

LIKE EMILY DICKINSON

Like Emily Dickinson
tucking tight little poems
into the corners and crannies
of her father's home
I tuck their names
into the crevices
of my crenelated heart.

Lonnie from Tennessee
smiling A-K amp
"Don't mean nothin'.
I got another one"

Danny from LA
unable to see
the last dawn we shared

Chief the Ute
willing himself to die
since he could not
will himself to live
a partial man

Pocho from Arizona
who wanted only that
the last words he heard
be in his mother tongue
words rightfully spoken
by his mother who,
absent, became me

Skeets from somewhere
who asked me to sing
Amazing Grace
because his mother did

The boy with no name
no voice
no face

All these and more
I tuck away
later to peruse
perhaps edit
perhaps to erase
at some leisure time
at penance time
sometime in a future
that leaves them behind

Emily in white,
I in green,
we do our work
endure and abide
tucking away the hurt
saving it for the time
when alcoves need airing
when corners need cleaning
when hearts need healing
when there are no more
empty corners
convenient to fill.

Dana Shuster
1968

DARK ANGEL

There's a white boy
crying in the darkness.
I'll be his mama tonight
and he won't care that my skin is black
cause he'll die
before dawn's early light.

I'm the Mexican's dark madonna
as the demerol goes in
but when he awakens
I'll be the bitch
who cut off the best part of him.

The Indian sees the Great Spirit
even though he has no eyes.
Fly away to the land
that has no reservations.
It's for both of us
my eyes will cry.

Black boy running in the big race
you'll never run again.
Your legs are gone
but you'll live on
wishing that now was then.

The smell of blood and sweat and fear
is soaking through my clothes.
Its copper taste is in my mouth
always in my nose.

I'll never wash that smell away.
There's not enough perfume
to cover up my time in hell
or that slaughterhouse of doom.

I know now what the slaves knew
that too much is still not enough
so I shine it on,
say it don't mean nothin'
'cause us black gals are tough.

Still I can't help but wonder
who is the enemy?
Is he yellow or black
red, brown or white?
Or could it be that it's me?

I'm so tired of being the leader
I don't want to decide who should die
I want to go home to my mama
Jesus help me or just let me die!

On the freedom bird I'm flying
their everywoman in the sky
I hear them call
try to save them all
with a touch and a little white lie.

Joan Arrington Craigwell
1990

MY WAR

Did I ever tell you . . . . . . how proud I was, ... of myself,
—for setting out to do *something*
—for not just sitting back and watching anymore
—for finding a way, with little regard for the consequences, to help out, to do my part, to stand alongside those suffering victims of war.
—for making my own statement about support, love and loyalty, even amidst the confusion about what it all meant.
—for having the guts to act, and not just ignore it anymore?
Did I ever tell you, what it meant to me . . . . The Vietnam War?

Did I ever tell you . . . . . how scared I was, ... for myself
—for the decision I'd made
—for the position I'd taken
—for the validity of my resolve, the appropriateness of my response, the effect on my family
—for my ability to be effective in the performance of my duties
—for my future, my strength and stamina, and my survival
—for whether the course I'd chosen was a mistake?

Did I ever tell you how embarrassed and ashamed I became to think that we'd all been taken,
—by a people who hated our presence, who took advantage of our caring, who laughed behind our backs and betrayed us in the night
—by a nation back home who didn't care, who went on with life as though we didn't exist, who'd written us off, who never noticed our return

—by a God who seemed to have deserted us all to suffer through, to die, to live alone with our pain forever?
Did I ever tell you what it meant to me. . . . . .The Vietnam war?

Did I ever tell you how we grew together, my new family and I,
   —how we stuck up for each other, laughed together to forget, lived as though it didn't matter how torn up we were becoming inside
   —how we knew nothing else would ever be the same again and no one else nor nothing else would ever have the intensity of meaning again
   —how we longed for home, "the World" and the old ways, but knew they no longer existed and hated to leave one another, although we never really said so
   —how we walked away from it all as though it never existed nor mattered, with all resolve to forget
   —how we never really could forget those who died, how we needed to cry but couldn't, how we never again felt "home" nor "family" in the way we did there, through the struggle and pain of Vietnam?
Did I ever tell you that?

Did I ever tell you how hard I tried and with what pride of accomplishment I did what needed to be done,
   —when the dying was too often, the bodies too hurt to repair, the grief beyond words and feeling
   —when babies cried and when they died
   —when the smells, the sounds of suffering and the recognition of lost limbs, function, health and life had to be dealt with in "kids" younger than
ourselves, ... 18, 19, 20, 21 and up–to ages beyond the years that we'd attained

—when the meaning of it all only came out . . .
. . . "hopeless, useless, and worthless. . . . a waste"?
Did I ever tell you what I felt?

Did I ever tell you about that part of me that was buried
somewhere within me for thirteen years after coming back
from Vietnam in 1971?

Did I ever tell you about being a nurse in a war . . . . My War?

Diane C. Jaeger
January 15, 1987

THE GIFT IN WARTIME

I offer you roses
Buried in your new grave
I offer you my wedding gown
To cover your tomb still green with grass

You give me medals
Together with silver stars
And the yellow pips on your badge
Unused and still shining

I offer you my youth
The days we were still in love
My youth died away
When they told me the bad news

You give me the smell of blood
From your war dress
Your blood and your enemy's
So that I may be moved

I offer you clouds
That linger on my eyes on summer days
I offer you cold winters
Amid my springtime of life

You give me your lips with no smile
You give me your arms without tenderness
You give me your eyes with no sight
And your motionless body

Seriously, I apologize to you
I promise to meet you in our next life
I will hold this shrapnel as a token
By which we will recognize each other

Tran Mong Tu
translated by Vann Phan
1969

WHERE ARE THEY NOW?

For weeks they hobbled and wheeled around me.
Healing from the wounds of war.

We fed, bathed, shaved, medicated,
stitched and unstitched their bodies.

We listened and counseled as pain poured from their souls.

If deemed healed in 30 days
back to battle they went,
to kill or be killed,
to live whole or maimed.

There is pain in not knowing what happened to them.
There is relief in not knowing what happened to them.

Margaret Flatt
1990

SECOND TOUR

Today was an ordinary day in the OR,
the usual allotment of train wrecks and gorks,
a sprinkling of crispy critters among
the occasional mix-'n-match and numberless gooks.

I remember a day when it wasn't so,
when the OR was nothing but chaos and carnage,
a day when I swore I would never see
mere train wrecks and gorks, crispy critters and gooks,
instead of people hurting more than I.

Sometimes I wonder: which day's casualty log bears my name?

Dana Shuster
1967

WOUNDS OF WAR

I

He walks off the chopper
bleeding.
In his relief at being out of the fire zone
    he has forgotten that he hurts
    or that he was in terror.

II

The shell fragment is too large
it has invaded his heart
    his lungs, his liver, his spleen.
He will not survive the night.

III

In order that another,
    who has a better chance,
    might survive,
she must remove this patient from life
    support equipment.
Her professional smile calms the other patients,
    hides the anguished murderer inside.

IV

Each wound receives the surgeon's scrutiny:
    this we will close, this we will drain,
    this entire area must be removed.
The eye surgeon, the chest surgeon,
    the orthopedist.
Each focuses on his own plot
forgetting for a time
    their common ground.

V

Infection sets in.
The wound becomes a greenhouse
for exotic parasitic growths.

VI

Wounds heal from the bottom up
        and from the outside in.
Each must be kept open,
        must be probed
        and exposed to light.
Must be inspected
        and known.

VII

She sits at the side of the road
offering to sell stolen oranges
        to the jeep riders passing by.
She does not name herself wounded.
Two rockets blew away her home
and rice paddy.
        Her husband is dead.
        Her son has been drafted.
        Her baby will never cry again.

VIII

He wheels his custom chair
    through the crowded bookstore.
He focuses on narrow aisles and tall shelves
   avoiding images
     of jungle trails and buried mines
     of leaving in the mud
       his legs
       and his left hand.

IX

In rage he shatters another window with his fist.
The glass shards never cut deeply enough
    to cleanse the guilt.

X

She is afraid to trust again.
Her days are haunted
    by the texture of blood
    the odor of burns
    the face of senseless death;
friends known and loved
    vanished
    abandoned.
She sits alone in the darkened room
    scotch her only hope.

XI

He stares at the gun he saved,
turning it over and over in his tired hands.
He is desperate to stop the sounds
    and the pictures.

XII

Wounds must be inspected
and known.
Must be kept open
and probed
and exposed to light.
Healing is from the bottom up
and from the outside in.

Marilyn McMahon
1988

VERMONT VIETNAM (I)

Hot summer day
on the River Road
swimmers of the Ompompanoosuc
dust in my eyes

      oh
      it is the hot wind from Laos
      the girl in Nhe An covers her face with a straw hat
      as we pass   she breathes   through cloth
      she stands between two piles of stone

      the dust of National Highway One blinds

me
summertime
I drive through Vermont
my fist on the horn, barefoot
    like Ching

Grace Paley
1971

SOME DAYS

Some Days
I can't help but remember
Who knows what triggers it today,
18 years later.
The game was war,
the prize survival
The toys were guns and tanks,
mortars and grenades.
White phosphorous.
I remember it well
A charred body: shades of black
shades of white.
A 10 year old boy
Dying.

War!
A term that conjures up visions:
of firefights and battlefields,
Not mass casualties,
traumatic injuries or triage.
Choppers!
The whirring reminder of life and death.
Damaged and disabled young men,
Brought to a different fight
The fight for one more life.
The struggle for one more day.

Some Days
I can't help but remember,
When these very young men,
without their arms or legs or
half of their faces,
looked to me for hope, encouragement

strength or peace.
When hidden behind my smile of,
"It'll be OK"
was the burden of the lie,
that knew that it wouldn't.

Anger! The Anger!
The silent, stoic anger.

The anger at the death
the anger at the carnage
the anger at the demands
that could not be met
the pain that could not be stopped
the wounds that could not be healed
the tears that could not be shed.

Yes, Some Days,
I can't help but remember:
standing there,
surrounded by beds
filled with young men
hearing the cries or
the whispered requests:
relief from the pain,
some moral support
a minute or two of
extra time.

But,
There never seemed to be
enough time—and
there never seemed to be
enough hands—and
there never seemed to be
enough me

to respond to the cries
and the sighs.

So soon I discovered
with no time for tears
Become numb to the pain,
Become numb to the cries,
Become numb to the death,
Walk away from the grief.

And Some Days
I can't help but remember
Reaching out to find a friend,
to hold a hand, to seek a peace
to find some respite
some respite from war.
Yet even then, I soon did learn,
that some would leave
and never come back
from their last fight or their last flight.
But I didn't call in sick in Vietnam
and I didn't say "I need a day off
'cause my friend just died."
After all, in Vietnam
Somebody's friend died everyday.

So I went on knowing
a part of my youth died every day
a part of my soul was lost.
Learning so clearly,
without a doubt
There's no such thing
as a respite from war.

And Some Days
I can't help but remember

That when I came home,
When I finally came home,
I came home to a life
that no longer was real.

Sometimes I tried to explain.
Other times I just stayed mute
feeling at first that they
wouldn't understand,
feeling really that they
didn't want to hear
knowing for sure that they'd
never really know.

Then I discovered that
I couldn't play.
Strangely I found
I forgot how to laugh
and amazingly enough
I didn't want to work.

Doctors didn't come on
The very first call
and I knew in Vietnam
That's all it would take
One call to say
"I need you here now."
And there they would be
as soon as I called;
because they knew if I said
"I need you here now,"
a life was at stake
or I wouldn't have called.

And Some Days,
I can't help but remember
realizing that
I really didn't care
that the lady down the hall
was complaining of pain
and wouldn't get up and
walk down the hall.
What right had she
to complain of such pain.
A gall bladder after all
was not the same pain
as the kind you get
from shattered legs,
and arms, and souls.

Yet I knew I was wrong
down deep somewhere.
But I also knew and
couldn't understand
why they didn't know
that people over there
were dying and dying
continually dying.
They didn't seem to know
and they didn't seem to care.
They seemed to think I should
be glad to be home,
when much to my surprise
I found that I wasn't.

Joan A. Furey
1987

THE "VIETNAM VET"

The "Vietnam Vet"
people instantly conjure
their own picture
in their mind

Is it ever of
a woman?
Huddled . . . somewhere . . .
alone
sleeping
trying desperately to shut out the world
that shut her out
or
that disappeared
as she reached out to trust it

Is it ever
that vision?
that woman?

Norma J. Griffiths
1982

OUR WAR

I don't go off to war
So they say
I'm a woman.
Who then
Has worn my boots?
And whose memories
Are these
Of blood, of burns
Of dressings and blank stares
Of heartaches, of sadness
Of duty, of love
and of honor.
I haven't known fear
Of rockets and mortars
And enemy guerrillas
So they say.
For I'm a woman
I don't go off to war.
Why then
Did I cradle you in my arms
Young soldier
As the lights went out
And deafening barrage
Crashed through my helmet
As chaos around
Left me burning
With anger and fear
As our hospital
Submits to attack
It's not noble
It's not fair
What are the rules?

These men have no weapons
As they lay suffering
Under steel beds
Is this their protection
Yes, and it's their hell
Man or woman
We are prey
To inhumanity
And to suffer
And survive together.
I'm a woman
And I have tasted
Man's hell—his war.
Our War.
I have taken his blood
his limbs and his life
to unknown places.
And he has asked
Nothing of me.
He knows
I'm a woman
And I am in his war
And that I love him
In no greater way
Than to care
And share in his
Life or his
Death.
But he knows
I cannot prevent
That unknown place
Called Heaven or Hell
He knows it better than I.
It is then I realize

His concern for me
As he says,
Nurse, how are you?
For he knows
I'm at war
And I'm a woman.
Please don't forget me
I've been through war's hell
And if only you'll listen
I've a story
Of young men and young women
and their valor
Who bled
For us all.

Diane Carlson Evans
1983

UNSEEN

I'm different from you veterans
I didn't carry guns
    Drop bombs
    Live on board ship.

But I was with you after Tet
    When you cried
    Were afraid to "patch" your mom to say you lost a limb—
    And wondered what your sweetheart would say.

Listened to your pain
When mail call brought "Dear John"

    learned the lingo of Nam:
        Hooch, slant eye, incoming, grunts.

Saw your jungle rot,
    Black Fever,
    broken bones, ugly burns,
    severed arteries,
    deep cavities where muscles had been.

    Saw you sweat,
    Heard you moan,
    Listened to nightmares while you slept.
    There on the wards, one open room.

We were bonded in that space
That cavern that has no place
In 1986.

This unseen veteran
    Shares your pain
    Feels the gap that has no name.

Mary O'Brien Tyrrell
1986

MONTAGNARD BRACELETS

He gave me two of his
Montagnard bracelets
When he was evac'd out
after his DEROS date.

I used to wear them a lot
And never paid much attention
To the spots that I thought
Were a flaw in the metal.

It was only last year
When I polished them
And part of the spot came off
That I realized
It was his blood.

Sara J. McVicker
1983

LOOK INTO MY EYES AND SEE

Look into my eyes and see
That I have known more than
A lifetime of misery.
At six or sixty
The face is still the same,
Aged and afraid to accept my destiny.
You come and go,
You weep for your own.
I too am an innocent of war,
Who cries for me?

Joyce A. Merrill
1987

JULY 20, 1969
. . . an introduction in 3 voices

In Seattle, almost 9:00 PM
after bedtime
for little girls
not quite fully dark.

                                        In DaNang, noon
                                        the next day.

On the moon . . .
day.

In Seattle, Mom and Dad
watched on their TV
4-year-old Shelley,
pleased at the chance
to stay up late,
snug in Mom's lap.
Janice, bored with waiting
read her book.
Front and back doors
propped open to catch
the breeze
off Salmon bay.

                                        In DaNang, 8
                                        guerrillas crept
                                        quietly to a make
                                        shift platform near
                                        Marble Mountain
                                        and aimed their
                                        launcher at the air

base for a foolhardy
daylight
attack on the
expected in-bound
plane.

On the moon, one man
stepped from a small
metal craft
bounced lightly on the
ladder, and out onto
the dusty ground.

Later, as Dad carried
his sleeping daughter
up to bed
as Mom closed the doors
and made a pitcher
of iced tea,
as Janice returned
to her book,

as the man on the moon
returned to his lander
for rest, water, food,

a squad of Marines
found the guerillas
foolish enough to
fire rockets in
daylight and shot
them all.

A Continental Airlines 707
which had been circling
for 2 hours
above the airstrip
waiting for the shelling
to stop,
landed.
163 American servicemen,
Commander Betsy Jackson
and I filed
down the ladder.

Marilyn McMahon
1990

DEATH SPEAKS

For so long, I welcomed death,
enticed it,
embraced it,
but always returned to the world
plucked, reluctantly, from its arms.

Now,
when I allow myself to feel the sorrow,
death taunts, moves closer,
seeming to grasp and clutch at my new life.

No longer welcome, it tells me:

"I am still here.
I, who carried so many from your arms;
I, brought close by the sound of chopper blades;
I, who grasped whom I wanted despite your efforts
        little woman, little girl, am death
        and whenever you think of Vietnam
        even if not of the wounded and dying
I, death, am there.

So, think of sunning on the beach at the Lep,
        and think of the Mateus you consumed in gaiety,
I, death, lurked behind the sun and held the bottle,
        to consume your youth,
        to age you by familiarity,
        and advance you rapidly
        to old age,
        and closer . . . to me!"

Norma J. Griffiths
1986

I HOLD THEM

Tossed together in a sea of dread
   Wound, injured, sick or dead
Thru monsoon rains and black of night
   Or, in Hell's own heat with sun burning bright
I hold them.

In thick red mud that turns to slime
   On hot white sand ground down with time
With broken bodies, racked with pain
   As unknown terrors rage through their frames
I hold them.

Borne by mothers, mourned by none
   Their future's past, their time now done
Calling out from depths of soul
   Pleading for hope to make them whole
I hold them.

Shattered faces, bodies, dreams and more
   Legs and arms fall to the floor
Their blood runs freely, mixed with mine
   And their last request, for just some time
I hold them.

Their questions plead, they don't request
   They demand to know they did their best
And as our eyes meet one last time
   While their fading souls meld in with mine
I hold them.

When it's all over and they breathe their last
   My heart is crushed, my mind locked fast
I hold them.

But the war's been done for twenty years,
   their faces blurred by long dried tears
As I find their names upon the Wall
   Fading and forgotten through the pall
I hold them.

Endless bodies that once held life
   Corpses produced by appalling strife
Through hopeless days and nights of pain
   As I seek a way to feel life again
I hold them.

They have become such a part of me
   When you look at me, who do you see?
Can I live if I set them free?
   Who will hold them
And salvage me?

Penny Kettlewell
1990

TO MY UNKNOWN SOLDIER BOY

Your bleeding wouldn't stop
the doctor kept yelling for blood
but I was frozen
your hand in mine
you kept calling for your mother.

I regret I didn't know you.
I can't tell your mother I was there.
Perhaps
she would feel some comfort.
I felt none.

I regret I didn't take your
dying, broken, dirt covered body
into my arms for her,
for you,
for me.

Your name, your unknown name
keeps running through my mind.

Your wounds,
your crying for help,
your pleading eyes,
will haunt me until
my own death.

It was only a matter of minutes,
then another wounded soldier
took your place.
Then another and another
and another.

Yet, perhaps
somehow
you knew I was there.
For you.

Mary Lu Ostergren Brunner
1984

DYING WITH GRACE

Did that eight-year-old boy,
racing gleefully into the playground,
black eyes shining with the joy
of kicking a soccer ball
ahead of him,
and met by two bullets
from an automatic machine gun,
did he die with grace?

Or his grandmother?
Who was rail-thin at 35
from too little food
and too many babies
and too much defoliant
and too few hopes,
who fell asleep in the refugee camp
and never woke up,
did she die with grace?

The white man in the suit and tie
on television
tells me that if I believe
in jesus
and in heaven
and jesus' love for me,
I can die with grace.

Could that be true?

The other white man
on television
tells us that this young man
once from Brooklyn
who fired his weapon
while struggling through the mud
on Hamburger Hill
or at Salerno
or deep in the Mekong jungle,
killing 12 of the enemy
before he was felled by a grenade,
that he died with grace.
The man calls it honor
and announces that his country
is proud of him.

An old man
once awarded the Silver Star
and Purple Hearts
and rank upon ranks
of honors and medals
dies of the cold in a park
across the street from the White House.
His death is not called graceful,
it is judged shameful
and it is named alcoholism.

And the woman
who wrote to the *San Francisco Examiner*
that finally, at the Vet Center,
she had found a way out
of nightmares
of choppers full of wounded
and dead
and flashbacks of nights torn
with mortars and rockets;
then could not live with her memories
and jumped from the Golden Gate Bridge.
Who is there to say that she died with grace
or did not?

Marilyn McMahon
1990

UNDER THE COVERS

I was always afraid
before,
that when I pulled down the covers
all I would see was
gaping holes
and blood.
And I never
pulled someone's hair
for fear it would be in my hand,
with the scalp and skull attached.

Now I explore your body
telling you that I'm counting the hairs
but really,
I'm caressing the curves and dents
and softness,
Proving to myself
that the horror isn't there . . .
on your body
under the covers.

Norma J. Griffiths
1986

WHEN THE PARADE PASSED BY

My dear friend,
you should have been there
when the parade passed by.

You would not have believed
the sights and sounds that violated your mind.
Didn't think we'd make it,
being there, counting time.

You should have been there
and seen the brilliant lights dancing from flares
that lit up the night.

You should have heard
the deafening thunder of a thousand storms
roaring in your ears while you hide,
then count faces and blessings.

You would have died
a million times over,
as you shook and searched your body for wounds,
and wondered if you were still alive.

You would have known
that deep inside you were dying,
a little at a time,
while yearning for a magic dressing
to cover the mortal wound in your soul.

You should have seen
the frailty and strength, life and death, hope and despair
that surged, then vanished
In the blink of an eye.

You would have cried
while swallowing every tear,
and kept it inside.

You should have felt
the indescribable joy of seeing half a smile
beaming from half a face,
or heard the groan and felt the grasp of a hand,
from one who was only another silent
and lifeless body.

You would have been proud
to see so much courage
in the face of overwhelming odds.

You would have wanted
to hold me and ease the pain,
if only for awhile.
Didn't think we'd make it, being there,
counting time, as the parade passed by.

You should have been there. . . .

Joyce A. Merrill
1987

IMAGES AT THE WALL

Rows and Rows of neatly engraved names
Strung across slabs of black granite
Names that once meant husbands, daughters, sons and lovers
Silent testament to the cost of the Vietnam war

I have walked at Gettysburg, Normandy and Verdun
Here I am not with history but with my own memories
Tho' your names have left me, your spirit never will
Yes I remember you

Young in the time of my youth
Believing in the time of my faith
Trusting in the time of my innocence
Never to see "The World" the same

The image of this black granite
Casts my face across your names
I am older now but you have never aged
Always young, always proud, America's best

Holding my hand is a daughter I never imagined then
Our images a curious convergence of the future on the past
Her generation is now America's shining hope
Endowed by our sacrifices—the sobering reality of war

Once we were children too
Growing up under the American Dream
Shocked by the streets of Dallas, wounded at Kent State
Set adrift in the Gulf of Tonkin

No one braced us for "shadow men" without their arms and
    legs
No one showed us how to celebrate a war we hadn't won
No one told us the taint of Agent Orange would seep to the
    unborn
No one warned us about the empty "Welcome Home"

The hard lessons of that war are etched in our hearts
Just as deeply as your names are engraved on this Wall
For we know that but for the hand of God
Our names would be here with yours

Linda Spoonster Schwartz
1986

I WENT TO VIETNAM TO HEAL

I went to Vietnam to heal
and came home silently wounded.
I went to Vietnam to heal
and still awaken from nightmares
about those we couldn't save.
I went to Vietnam to heal
and came home to grieve for those
we sent home blind, paralyzed,
limbless, mindless.
I went to Vietnam to heal
and discovered I am not God.

To you whose names are on this wall
I am sorry I couldn't be God
If I were God, if there were a God,
there would be no need for such a wall.

But I am not God, and so I go on
seeing the wounded when I hear a
chopper, washing your blood from my hands,
hearing your screams in my sleep, scrubbing
the smell of your burned bodies from my clothes,
feeling your pain, which never eases,
fighting a war that never ends.

Dusty
1985

CONFESSION

Day before First Friday
we file from our classroom to the church
at our assigned time.
"Bless me, Father,
for I have sinned.
It has been one month
since my last confession:
I was angry with my little sister
I was jealous of her new doll.
I was selfish, and did not share
my roller skates.
I was proud, and I boasted."
In that dark cozy place,
my eyes are tightly closed.
Father does not know
who I am.
A blessing, the Sign of the Cross.
I march to the altar rail,
gaze bent to the floor.
I kneel, hiding my eyes in my knuckles.
Three Hail Marys, and the Act of Contrition.
I am forgiven.
My soul is pure white.
Tomorrow, I may receive Holy Communion.

Sunday morning Mass
after ten hour night shift
admissions, transfers, two deaths.
Armpits still chilled from warming
frozen plasma.
Fingernail stained orange-
Betadine prep for an emergency trach.

—— 118 ——

We sit wearily in metal folding chairs.
Bright, sun-filled quonset hut:
the Chapel of Saint Luke.
Slowly we stand as the priest
and his attendants file in.
We bow our heads,
one sign of the cross
sketched in the air.
My silent catalogue:
Bless me Father, for . . .
I was enraged, wanted to hurt another.
I committed adultery two, no, three times.
I was proud, would not pray.
Thirty others forgiven at the same time.
Our souls are purified
we may receive Communion.

Night
the black hour
when sleep has fled again.
Poison gas in Iran and Iraq.
In El Salvador, disembowelled priests
and two women.
Star Wars
and Minutemen.
Martinis and handshakes in Beijing
across one thousand bodies.
Blockades create starvation
and democracy.
Arms shipments.
I am enraged
and frightened of my rage.
I am appalled
and made helpless.

I am guilty of fear
helplessness
failure to believe or hope
having believed and having
asked no questions.
Where is forgiveness
and purification of soul?
Where is communion? and when?

The dark, private cubicle is empty
door closed tight.
The sun-filled chapel
was blown up by those
who believed in a different god.
Knuckles can no longer provide
a safe dark.
I will not pray.

Marilyn McMahon
1990

IV
AWAKENING

"There is nothing more intimate than sharing someone's dying with them. When you've got to do that with someone and give that person, at the age of nineteen, a chance to say the last things they are ever going to get to say, that act of helping someone die is more intimate than sex, it is more intimate than childbirth, and once you have done that you can never be ordinary again."

Dusty, Army Nurse
Vietnam
1987

"I needed to find other women who knew what I knew, and more. I needed to talk to women who had seen unspeakable things, who were without self-pity, who had faced the liars and lunatics, who had survived all of it and, in surviving, made a difference."

Gloria Emerson, Journalist
Vietnam
1972

BEING A VET IS LIKE LOSING A BABY

Being a vet
Is like
Losing a baby

No one says
Anything to you
And you don't
Say anything to them.

Lily Lee Adams
1981

COMBAT ZONE

The conflict has never stopped.
My mind's a battlefield where
There is no treaty.
I remember Lynn
Who camouflaged efficiency
In a lyric voice and sweetness.
RED ALERT
Barb could drink the strong
Under the table
So they couldn't see her exit
In a purposeful stride.
CONDITION YELLOW
Emily rarely spoke
And when she did
It was literary, intellectual,
And sometimes in Flemish.
FIRE FIGHT
I stole woman pictures from them all.
It doesn't matter now
They're locked in a DMZ.
A minefield protects their discovery
While war ravages my soul.

Kathleen Trew
1970

CRYING

I'm doing it again.
Crying.
It doesn't take much
To set it off these days.
This time it was a letter from Joanie
With some of her poetry.

I tell myself it's worse when I'm tired.
But that's not so.
It's when I let myself feel
And remember.

Sara J. McVicker
1983

UNNAMED

Oh silent one inside of me, how dare you come around.
How dare you speak, how dare you shriek, how dare you
   breathe a sound
of horrors that we witnessed then, amidst the frantic pace
of twisted limbs and broken forms, and anguish in each face!

A million scenes of shattered dreams, young lives and goals
   and souls,
just swept away without a sound, to rest beneath their knolls.

You promised to be silent, to live your life within
the gloomy depths of memory, and never to begin
the torment that I've left behind, in pieces of my soul,
in bits of me I've long forgot, in parts that make me whole.

How dare you come around again, how dare you say my name.
How dare you speak, how dare you shriek, how dare
   you . . . but you came!

Diane C. Jaeger
1987

DO YOU REALLY WANT TO KNOW

Do you really want to know
how you can help me?
Then don't turn your back on me
as if I was to blame!
You share in this too.
I did the dirty work,
the least you can do is
listen to me.

Bobbie Trotter
1981

HINDSIGHT

"Why write about it now?"
My thirteen year old asks.

What difference does it make
What bearing on her life?
Reared in this home
    With a Dad who visits weekends.

I wonder
    If her parents met in Duluth, instead of Guam
        Taking a break in Naval uniforms,
        The idyllic Pacific creating a mood
        On this island eight miles wide.
        The wounded men and P 52's,
        Military maneuvers, geographical bachelors,
        A need to be close.

The nurses' quarters hummed with distractions:
    News from home
    Twiggy fashions
    China for hope chests
    Glen Campbell in stereo
    Thursday night happy hour.

Some nurses cracked and disappeared
From humid tropical weather
80 bed wards, sans air conditioning.
The wounds, the waste, the loss.

I re-read those letters sent home
No mention there of war and pain,
Casualties and stress.

I need to write it now.

Mary O'Brien Tyrrell
1986

SAIGON?

If one more guy
asks me if I was in Saigon
or DaNang
I think I'll scream.
Or maybe pop him in the nose.
That's what male vets do to get rid of their frustrations.

They don't realize
How much it hurts
That THEY don't even know.

I've read so much about them.
Couldn't they learn something
About me?

Sara J. McVicker
1983

EVEN NOW

Even now,
after twenty years,
I still feel
abandoned and forgotten,
uncounted,
unnumbered.
Left to change all alone
in an airport Ladies Room.
    "You go over there"
Go to the corner and wash
the mud and the blood.
Forgotten, silenced and cast away
for over two decades
and now I can't deal with
the newly kindled interest.
"Did you see Sixty Minutes?"
And I want to scream and
rip off their faces:
where was your interest
and empathy over the past
twenty years? . . .
Buried out back
with your old dead dog?

                     Bernadette Harrod
                     1989

CONFESSIONAL

I jealously guard my pain
as if I alone
can own the horror of Vietnam.
In the private confessional
of my heart
I will not part with the nameless memories
. . . kid with blownout spinal cord
. . . triple amputee bed three
. . . freckled face no whiskers no penis
   virginity forever lost
   to the hateful whore Bouncing Betty
Who are they?

What voyeurs want to hear
how I loved them
sent them away
chose to forget their names
bury them
in the dark grave of my dead soul?
Who are they?

Bless me, fathers, for I have sinned
Bless me, mothers, for I have sinned
Bless me, children, sisters, brothers
For I have sinned.
It has been twenty years since my last confession
Forgive me for the arrogance
of my silence.

Lou McCurdy Sorrin
1990

THE WALK TO THE WALL

I approached the wall with hesitation and fear
That flowed through my arms and my legs and my heart
To that place in my soul that had brought me here,
Here for the walk, the walk to the wall.

I continued to walk, to walk to the wall, knowing of one,
One name to be found. One name at that moment
Clamored my brain, I had waited so long to tell him goodbye
His name screamed out as I walked to the wall.

I said I remember his name it seems, I have always
remembered
His name, over all these years I remember his name.
I don't know why I remember the name
It's just always been with me, the name, I recall.

I approached the wall, the panels, the names, looking,
looking
In May, '69. There were so many names in May, so many
But I knew of the day, the 17th of May
I had written the poem then, then on that day.

I turned and I said I can't find it but I know,
I know it must be here, here on the wall, you see
The poem; I wrote the poem the day he died, 17 May in '69.
I have it with me to share you see, I wrote it then,
Then on that day.

I heard you say the man over there, there with the book,
He has all the names. Tell him the name, the name you know.
I turned to the man with the name I knew, I said Edward K.
On 17 May in '69, Pleiku, I remember, I remember the name.

— 133 —

I looked at the man and I heard him say, Here
It's here, the name, it's here, it's there on the wall.
Look on the west on panel 24 line 85, yes that's
The name, where the name is engraved, line 85 on the west,
The west of the wall.

I walked to the west, to the west of the wall
I looked at the panels, so many were there as parts of the wall.
You said 85, I've found it, it's here, the name you remember
I found it, it's here.

I stared at the wall, on the west, on the wall
I saw it right there, the name on the wall.
I sank to my knees in the dirt near the wall with
The rose I had brought clutched to my soul.

I looked at the wall, at the name on the wall, I looked and
I cried and I cried at the wall, in the dirt as you held me
And hugged me and helped me to cry.
I thought of the boy with the name on the wall.

I cried on your shoulder in front of the wall, I whispered
So softly the name on the wall and I said as you held me
So close to your heart, I said very softly in a whisper
So hoarse, that young man with his name etched in the stone
Taught me all I need know about war and this wall.

We walked from the wall with our arms still entwined.
We walked down the path in silence and peace.
From the wall, yes we walked
Sharing our pain and our grief.

I thank you my friend for the walk to the wall
And your help and your Love, you looked out for your friend;
When she walked to the wall, to the west of the wall,
In search of a name, a name on the wall.

Joan A. Furey
1983

WHERE'S THE TRIPWIRE, JACK?

Where's the tripwire, Jack?
I know you found it, because I saw your body
cold and gray
drained of blood
on the floor.

Where's the tripwire, Jack?
What did you see in those last moments?
What did you think?
What did you feel?

We were close, Jack—sometimes so close
that when you chewed, I swallowed.
We were buddy close,
lover close,
twin close,
friend close.
So, friend, why didn't you warn me?

Where's the tripwire, Jack?
You must have carried it in your head
all the way back from that unspeakable time,
that suffering place
to lie in wait
for a vulnerable day
for a careless moment
to maim forever and ever your future
to stain forever and ever your dreams
to soil forever and ever your spirit
to rend forever and ever your soul

Did I carry that same tripwire back
with me?
Is it waiting in my dreams?
Is it hiding behind a memory?
We were so close, Jack, it must be so.
Where's the tripwire, Jack?

I look for your name on this Wall, Jack.
It's not here—but it should be.
We are war casualties, all, Jack.
Our names aren't here, Jack,
but our spirits burden the air,
palpable in mourning,
tense in waiting, watching.
Waiting, watching for the tripwire, Jack—
for the tripwire.
Like they say, Jack,
Time is a motherfucker.

Dusty
1989

CRONE

In each woman lives the voice
of her mothers   the survivor
the one she will become   the crone

The polished granite
facing the names
shutting out people
eyes   tired of searching
for one name that might be familiar
skin   taut with tears
unshed   for the faces without names.
Unable to move.

An old woman moves close
her sleeve brushing mine
in the black mirror
she is short, wears a brown
coat of warm wool
a knit hat pulled snugly over her ears.

She squints in the glare
bifocals
is she looking for a name?
She peers at my face
in the mirror.
Why does she look at me?
Perhaps my reflection covers
the name of her son
or grandson.

I must move, old woman
I do not want your grief.

Tell me   do you know a name here?
do you get to put a face
a smile   a curl
on one of these names?
are your tears
for a child you once held?

I can see the wounds, old woman
and the blood   the faces   the eyes
I do not know to which names they belong.

I want to move
but I stand   frozen in her gaze.
Through the lines
in her cheeks
the tears spill   shining
from the bright
surface of the wall.
I am trapped   I must move
her tears hold me.
She has not reached out
to touch the letters
as so many do
only her left sleeve rubbing my elbow.

The silence of her tears
no other sound.   I
will not speak   or cry out
I want to leave   I am held
by her elbow   her face.

Does she know
I cannot recall their names?

I will not cry here
where tourists will think
me a widow
or an abandoned lover.

That grief is for you, old woman
not me.

Surely you would leave
if you could see the anger
rubbing elbows   can't you feel it?
Aren't you afraid of my rage?
        why did they die?
        why didn't I stop it?
        why can't I remember their names?
why haven't you moved away?

These bitter tears.

Her short wide hand strokes
the reflection of my face
her elbow, firmly now, is pressed against
my arm.   I do not see
fear in her   or anger.
Her tears have stopped.

She waits   eyes locked
watching my tears
still
waiting.

Marilyn McMahon
1990

—— *140* ——

IT'S BEEN SO LONG

I have an elusive friend
Called death, a companion
Of mine I cannot send away
I've tried, but it haunts me
With faces and blown
Away dreams of young
Soldiers and Vietnamese
I did not ask for this friend
It was born to me in
Vietnam, naked with truth
And terror and peace
And named mortality
O' friend, please go away
You robbed me of innocence
So many years ago
You make me feel so old
You rob me of laughter and fun
In Vietnam, death friend
You had the power to release
The pain and lead lives to
Eternity, don't haunt me
Any longer with those
Memories and faces, I know
I cannot suffer for them now
Please leave me alone
In war's insanity you
Stole a part of me
The part that feels dead
Stolen in my youth I
Want it back now, O' friend
Fourteen years late
It's been so long

Diane Carlson Evans
1983

SHORT 1968–1990

See how I strut
and sashay my butt
just a bit.
Walking with the short stick
Jake gave me when he left.
Can't talk.
I'm too short.
Thinking about wearing a miniskirt
perfume
long hair
being a round-eyed girl
back home.
I'm short
I'm short
I'm short
Why is it taking so long?

Lou McCurdy Sorrin
1990

V
HEALING

"Vietnam isn't behind us at all; it's in us. Sometimes it is only a shard of memory; sometimes it is a ferocious trauma. It defined one generation and influenced those that preceeded and followed. To understand it, we need to think about it and feel it; the memorial is the one place we have in common where those feelings can be expressed. Until we go there, we are, in a sense, incomplete, and so is the memorial."

Laura Palmer, Journalist
Vietnam
1987

"I had still not grown accustomed to seeing people torn and bleeding and dying in numbers like these. When one patient dies, it is agonizing enough; when you are faced with such mass suffering and death, something cracks inside of you, and you can't ever be quite the same again."

Juanita Redmond, Army Nurse
Bataan—WW II
1943

HOW DO YOU SAY GOODBYE?

How do you say goodbye
when you've never said hello?
Stand in front of that black marble wall
see in your reflection their names,
then touch them.
You will say hello and goodbye
together.

Penni Evans
1984

"THANKS, NURSE"

November 13th, 1982
I stand beside the Vietnam Veterans Memorial.
Pleiku, is written on my wrinkled jungle hat, and
71st Evacuation Hospital, Vietnam.
Wearing it today feels natural
Even with a skirt and among strangers.
Thirteen years ago it found its place
In a foot locker with worn out combat boots,
Fatigues, a malaria net and poncho liner.
Strange memorabilia for a young woman of 22 years.
A foot locker filled with memories
Of a lifetime of one year and
Locked away, forever—I had hoped,
Until today.

"Thanks, Nurse," that day in Washington, D.C.
You, with your boonie hat and
Faded camouflage
Threw your arms around me, and said
"Thanks, nurse, I never had a chance to say that"
The tears rolled down my face,
Don't make me cry,
I've passed thirteen years without a tear.
Please, don't remind me of sadness
With that look on your face.
My soul was overwhelmed with
Emotion I hadn't felt
Since leaving that faraway war
In 1969.
"You nurses saved our lives, you know, we
Love you,"
My tears are uncontrollable, and
I am as much with the
Dead as with the living.

Facing the wall, I encounter
Something I left behind me so many
Years ago.
I am at that moment lifted away
And reunited with those who suffered
And died and had left me
Alone.
Left me alone, with the memories of them.
And left me too numb to cry.
As I put my hands on the hard granite
And touched the names of those who
Died, 1968—'69, I no longer
Felt alone.

Those who had died, came back
at that moment,
Allowed me to grieve, embraced me
And touched a part of my
Soul I had thought was gone.
That vague place in my Life,
Vietnam, which could not bring forth
Emotion or feelings
Or tears.
It was such a relief to cry now, to
Feel again. It was so strange.
I felt unbearable sadness, and yet
Set free—free of an intangible
Burden.

That beautiful black granite
Wall, now carries the burden
For me
And for us all.
It carries the names and souls,
The memories, of those who died
In Vietnam.
It shelters them with respect
And dignity.

"Nurse, I don't want to die here," they would say
"Will I make it home? Oh God, don't let me die here."
That look in their eyes—so young, so serious,
Please don't make me remember.
The longing for home among the
Wounded was so strong.
We worked so hard to "get them home."
And thousands we did,
But for those who died we were
Sorry they couldn't have their last wish.

It would not have been their
Last wish—to be on this wall
Their life had just begun—
"Nurse I want to get home."
Now they are home and
Are again with their fallen
Friends.
The memorial that honors the living
And the dead, by giving us
a Place
To join together.

To you in your faded camouflage
And boonie hats and
Green berets, I want to say

"Thank you" too, from someone who
Cared for you in Vietnam, and
Still cares today, "Thank you, too"
For you see, you, and this wall
Set me free
Free to cry and free to remember,
What I had hoped to forget
And found I could not.

If our country could have known
But one dying man, alone in Vietnam
With that look on his face
And hopelessness in his eyes
If this country could have seen
The courage he had and concern
For his friends
If this country could have
Wept in his tears
And told him he was good.
If only, this country would have
Listened—listened and learned of his
Experience and his sacrifice
And then told him they were
Proud. If only there would have been
"Thanks."

We sacrificed our youth
I'm not sure why
How does one explain, to those
Who didn't go
The fear, the suffering, the inhumanity,
It's not what we wanted
To have names on this wall.
Or to visit a Place such as this, but

It was a real war
And we are real veterans.

Now this country has wept
In our tears from that era
By watching us stand proudly, honorably, beside
The Names, our comrades.
Sons and daughters at war do not know why
They are chosen ones to sacrifice.
But we stand proud and we will not
Let our nation forget our
Comrades.

Diane Carlson Evans
1983

WE WENT, WE CAME

We went to the war;
We came back to chaos.
We went with the values of healing and caring;
We came back with the hatred for a nation.
We went believing in a just cause;
We came back suspicious of our great leaders.
We went thinking our young bodies were immortal;
We came back knowing we were used and fragile.
We went innocent and forgiving;
We came back embittered and intolerant.
We went alone and open;
We came back alone and isolated.
We went whole and unwise;
We came back fragmented and wise.
We went to the Wall;
We came back away with hope.

Janet Krouse Wyatt
1986

REUNITED

I came upon the veteran, about two years ago.
She probably was in there, though, long before "Hello."
I don't know where she came from, nor where she hopes to go.
I only know I've missed her—the memories now aglow.

I didn't always like her, in fact I shied away
from letting her express herself, in any worthwhile way.
She never got upset with me nor seemed to mind or say,
"You really should acknowledge me, you know the price I
    pay."

Why did she come to meet me then, why did she reappear?
Why can't I now ignore her like I did for all those years?
Why does she make me listen to stories she's held so dear?
Why does she keep persisting, when she sees it draws my
    tears?

I came upon the veteran, about two years ago.
She's been locked up inside of me, so no one else would know.
I tried to hide her presence, the pain and anger slow,
The bitterness, the feeling used, the grief, that hurt me so.

It's good to have her back again, it's best to have her near,
to where I can discuss with her the many things we fear.
The way we used to act as though we didn't even hear,
the talk of the distant Vietnam Wall they built, and the
    dedication year.

And then we went to Washington, and later to New York.
We sat atop the wall and cried and lost the bottle's cork.
We waded into memories of people we'd forgot,
and now we sit and meditate about the War we fought.

I really do believe she'll stay—the veteran in me.
She says she's really weary and it's good to be let free.
I don't know how we'll co-exist, with values all askew,
But one thing is for certain, that we'll find one way, not two!

Diane C. Jaeger
1986

OUR OWN PARADE

You wait twenty years for your own parade;
Until the reasons begin to fade.
So you go ahead and give your own;
For the seeds and weeds you've already sown.

Down the road we trod;
Alone we go, alone we come.
When we were few and so afraid;
We were able to give our own parade.

The horns and drums were silent;
The nation had been rent.
Across the land, voices cried;
For brothers and sisters—all who died.

Down the road we trod;
Alone we go, alone we come.
When we were few and so afraid;
We were able to give our own parade.

The battered flag refused to fly;
We couldn't help but wonder "why?"
Budding pride was just a sign;
As we crossed the darkened line.

Down the road we trod;
Alone we go, alone we come.
When we were few and so afraid;
We were able to give our own parade.

Janet Krouse Wyatt
1988

IN WAR AND PEACE

flooded with feelings
of peace and love
a sense of completion
shared
with those who know
the pain and fear
of the process
we've gone through
from beginning to
a never ending
sense of purpose
lost for so long
in confusion and doubt
now gone lifted from me
in the camaraderie of reunion
the laying of a simple wreath
the placement of a small pin
the embrace of an old friend
and the tears of a no longer young man
saying: "Hey Pleiku '69—Remember March
Thanks for pulling me through"
I love you all of you
Men and Women
joined together
in War and Peace

Joan A. Furey
1984

MY LETTER TO THE WALL—
NOVEMBER 1989

I'm the one who was wounded by your shrapnel.
I'm the one you gave your life for.
I'm the one who stole your wallet.
I'm the one you sometimes didn't pay for the night.

I'm the one you took your anger out on.
I'm the one you came to for comfort.
I'm the one you sometimes called Lisa or Brenda.
I'm the one who would be whatever you wanted me to be.

I'm the one who made fun of your feelings.
I'm the one who held you when you were afraid.
I'm the one who made you happy when everything was so
    crazy.
I'm the one who hurt you sometimes when I didn't know any
    better.
I'm the one you thought had no feelings, but I do.

I'm the one who was there with you.
I'm the one you left behind.
I'm the one who survived.
I'm the one who learned about life through your death.

I'm the one who learned about feelings through memory of
    you.
I'm the one who learned about you too little too late.
I'm the one with all this knowledge and wisdom because you
    touched my life.
I'm the one who feels cheated because you are not here to
    share that with.

I'm the one who didn't have the chance to tell you I am very
    sorry.

I'm the one who didn't hold it against you.
I'm the one you probably don't remember,
But I remember you.
I'm the one who is part of you
And you are part of me.

Not one second goes by in my life that I do not speak to you
    in my heart.
That I do not think of you silently in my heart,
And thank you for your deaths so that I can be here.
I'm the one who wants you to be happy and satisfied.

Because I'm alive and I can feel.

Nguyen Ngoc Xuan
1989

AT PEACE

Now I feel at peace with myself
All the anger has left
It was the sediment
At the bottom of the bottle
That I couldn't reach
But I finally got it out.

Lily Lee Adams
1981

GUIDED JOURNEY

In the name of the Lord Jesus Christ
    I baptize thee young woman,
Veteran of many wars
    both personal and public.

Attacking and retreating and
    revealing and reversing,
Walls of death, of dignity,
    of defiance and denial;

Lay now scattered at my feet
    destroyed, disjointed or diffused.
Seeking simple sanity in quiet sleep
    in peace and dreams,

Reaching out to touch the heart,
    to hold the hand, to reach the soul,
Of simple truths and revelations
    cautiously unfolded.

Confronting both the good and bad
    the beautiful and ugly,
The personal paths and personal pain
    the fear, the rage, the sorrow.

Unable to reverse this flow of thought,
    of hurt, of feeling;
I kicked the walls, I cursed my God,
    I lived a time quite silent.

And then I cried, and cried, and cried,
    afraid I'd never stop,
Frightened that I'd drown my life
    in swirling seas of sadness.

Yet hanging on to one fine thread
    of trust and love and patience
I found within a source of strength,
    of warmth, of hope, of purpose.

I watched the pictures passing by,
    the flashes of the past;
The haunted looks, the staring eyes,
    the ever present shouting whys.

I felt the pain, released the rage,
    I cried the tears of sorrow.
A troubled past, a painful path,
    A frightened child grasping;

Soon released, revealed, renewed,
    we cleared that cluttered path
Of shattered myths and broken dreams,
    of dragons, dinosaurs, and doubts.

So now I see a lighted way,
    I see the birds, the butterflies,
I see the sun, the sky, the moon,
    The stars, the light, the rays, the hope.

I feel the warmth, the joy, the peace
    that comes with quiet restful sleep.
I see, I feel, I cry, I laugh. I love
    today; I live each day.

This gift bestowed upon my life,
   freedom from fear and faith restored
So once again I kneel to pray, I bow
   my head, I quietly say:

Thank you God
   for this gift,
      Today.

Joan A. Furey
1984

VI
LESSONS

"I ache over Vietnam. I ache because it was such a beautiful country and we managed to cream the crap out of it. We didn't stop to learn about the culture, we didn't ask the peasants what they wanted, we didn't or wouldn't think. We made beggars out of an entire nation—a nation of very proud people—and then turned around and said, 'Ha! Look at these beggars!' We didn't think for one minute that the people of Vietnam had any rights. We didn't even think they were human—it was 'Gooks don't bleed, gooks don't feel pain, gooks don't have any sense of loyalty or love.' And you know, we're making the same sickening mistakes (again) . . ."

Gracie Liem, American Civilian
Vietnam, Cambodia
1987

"I hope my son Jonathan never has to go, but I would be a fool to sit here and say that he won't. That's the way it's going to be. And I understand now, and I've got to learn to live with it."

Elizabeth Allen, Army Nurse
Vietnam
1990

GRANDFATHERS ROCKING

Grandfathers rocking on sagging front porches
spinning out glories of battles long ended
Horrors unmentioned and screaming forgotten
Eager belief spelled on tiny new faces
Babies who dream as they're tutored to dream
Male bonding rituals of ancient lineage.

Is this the way it is vectored through time,
this fervor to offer their anonymous blood
in the name of the powerful, the prophet, the mighty,
in the name of dark urges most dare not articulate?
Or is it perhaps a Y-linked pandemic
never isolated because researchers are male?

Grandmothers wonder in sweltering kitchens
as they prepare supper for one less than before.

Dana Shuster
1990

KEEP MUM

Teach 'im ta fight.
Teach 'im ta run.
'E's doin' a duty.
Wot mus' be done.

Giv 'im a gun.
The blood mus' run.
Tis honor and glory
wot mus' be won.

Tell 'im it's freedom.
Tell 'im we've won.
But 'bout the horror,
keep mum, keep mum.

Norma J. Griffiths
1986

FLASHDANCE

The sad glad plastic bags
flashing past my eyes flicker
as they pass the past
passes flashing fast
from here to there from there to here

The green plastic masks
the tasks leading to the
depths of death arranged
in silent, sorrowful rows
disguised as someone else's trash

But I can see beyond the flash
the flickering flaw found in the sound
of a young man's scream
surrounded by the flashdance
of death, destruction and devastation
as one man's duty is done.

Joan A. Furey
November 1, 1983
(following Beirut bombing)

MY DEAD ARE NOT SILENT

My dead are not silent.
They scream in my dreams.

My dead are not still.
They reach for their mothers.

My dead are young soldiers
spent, wasted, discarded.

They paid the price
for political ploys
for strategic follies
for tactical errors.

The politicians and planners
the orderers and senders
discomfited but unshamed
demand that my dead lie quiet
that my grief be smothered
that my ache be shunned
that my memories be denied.

But my dead will not be stilled
They will not be shelved
numbered
catalogued
straightened
into sanitized rows.
Their blood yet drips through my soul
Their moans still echo through my heart.

My dead demand remembrance
My dead demand honor
My dead demand that lessons be learned.
I hear them still
through my dreams
through my laughter
through my prayers

How can I make you hear?

Dana Shuster
1986

CORDWOOD

Cordwood Bodies stacked up high—
For them it's over—they don't cry—
Dark plastic bags zipped up tight—
They've lost the battle, lost the fight—

But we're still here—condemned to stay—
To fight the memories that rage today—
For safety's sake, we've zipped our shells.
To hide in our worlds of living hells.

'Cause we've *all* lost this war we couldn't win—
The legacy passed on to our next-of-kin—
May they be the wiser, discern the lies
That give us Cordwood Bodies stacked up high.

Penny Kettlewell
1990

IN THE WAR ZONE

In the war zone
there are no heroes.
The king and his court
name heroes
give awards and medals.
But listen to the criteria
for HERO in a war:
      1. killing many of those named enemy
      2. often, while dying.
A dead hero is a lie.

In the war zone
there are many jesters
clowns with sad faces
impossible, implausible roles.
One laughs at the jester
in order to not cry.
One becomes a jester
in order to not know
of the urge to cry.

In the war zone
there are many who are called
guides.
Along their path is obedience
ritual
tradition.
Clean uniforms to which mud
does not stick.
Salutes.
Medals. Ribbons.
Flags on the coffin.

Taps.
The guided often die.
The guides do not.

In the war zone
there are no guardians.
Your angel has stayed at home
next to your bed
where once you prayed
each night.

In the war zone
there are saints.
In the church of war and sacrifice
martyrs are saints.
A dead hero is a saint.
Pray to your last sergeant
that you will be wounded
just enough to go home
but not enough to hurt.
If it happens
you will know
that the sergeant
is now a saint.

Who are the villains
in the war zone?
If a villain is one who acts
contrary to the public good
then all in the war zone
are villains.
Except the children.
But remember that children
act only to survive.

In the war zone
the madonnas
are pictures in a wallet
or they are dead women
suckling infants
in the ditch at the side of the road.

The king and his court
the queen and her women
do not go to the war zone.
Occasionally a knight
leaves the table to give
the war zone the grace
of his presence.

There is mud in a war zone
and blood
arms and legs left behind
hungry children
burned fields
burned homes.
Frightened people in the ditches
numb people in the trenches
angry people in the streets
lonely people in the bars
shattered people in the hospitals
and unmarked graveyards.

There are many, many body bags
in the war zone.

Marilyn McMahon
1988

—— *173* ——

POEM WITHOUT NAME

Flares fall
Illuminating the horizon
Over there, so many bombs and guns
Tomorrow, so many corpses.
The flares keep falling

Drops of tears, oh tears.
He died
Yesterday he was still there
Rifle in hand, dreaming.
My lips are smooth with tears.

Where do you come from?
City or countryside?
Why didn't we say hello
Why didn't we say "How are you?"
You from the northern mountains or the southern jungles.

Why do you shoot each other?
Why lay those mines?
How many have died! And what for?
Who doesn't have a heart?
Who doesn't dream to be a bird?

Why isn't your blood red anymore?
Perhaps it's too windy
Tomorrow the field green with grass
Will cover a boyfriend's corpse.
Oh, what a lonely tomb.

Oh Heaven! Please let the day come soon
When flares stop falling
When enemies disband
For who is the enemy?
Only people fight people.

Oh Heaven! I wish it would rain harder
So the flares can't fire
So the bullets can't strike
So nothing can destroy our homes. Oh please!
So the helicopters can't fly.

You make jokes in Vietnamese
When something makes you feel pleased
But I cry in Vietnamese
When I feel sad
For someone else or even for myself.

Think of our beautiful native land.
Turn your face and look
Before you destroy everything.
The land can be green everywhere,
With a girl's light-flying blouse over yonder.

Minh Duc Hoai Trinh
1974
Translated by Phan Thanh Hao with Lady Borton

(*Note*: This poem was written in 1974, after the American withdrawal,
when only Vietnamese fought with Vietnamese.)

SNAFU

For the lifers

The God-Squad smoked dope
The priest was a closet gay
The Top Sergeant dealt in whores
For lost lonely soldiers to lay
. . . Innocence was not a character
In this play

Kathleen Trew
1970

THE GENERAL'S CAR

I first saw
the dark tinted windows of the car.
Then the red license plate
with only one star.

Hardly worth re-arranging what I was carrying

To give him the finger.

Norma J. Griffiths
1982

FROM THIS DISTANCE I TALK TO YOU

In this land of fire I think of you
The way the sail on the sea misses the port.
Here the land is cracked everywhere
But my love for you is whole.

As I write to you
The artillery explode overhead.
The atmosphere is frenzied with this bombing raid
Moon beams boil in the explosions
Rach Bap, Dong Du—all are flames.
The day here is so long
Time melts into endlessness.
The earth is hot, waiting for the next battle
(But this minute I devote just to you.)

Whenever the moon rises over the Saigon River
No boats venture onto its immense waters.
The banks of bamboo trees are burnt, battered
No couples dare stroll along a village road
Here, happiness must be silent.
Missing, waiting with no promise of meeting.
Love is seen in calm eyes
Amidst the threat of death every night.
Here, in the tunnels
Life continues amidst our comradeship
Love is by words
As we share rice and manioc.
No one mentions former happiness.

The future is so clear and simple.
Night will pass and day will come.
The land is burnt, but it will again grow green.

Some day, if I can ever live with you
I'll not be angry with you as
I have been in the past.
Life teaches me that amidst blood and fire
I can never think of having
The happiness I used to imagine.

Ha Phuong, Cu Chi
1974
(Translated by Phan Thanh Hao with Lady Borton)

SEVENTEEN SUMMERS AFTER VIETNAM

eyes closed, lying on a Maine beach
listening to the ocean, sound of
choppers coming in. Flashback.
Alpha Bravo Charlie
composites of a dream

Whiskey Yankee Zulu
phantasms of the expendable lives
of my generation wasted in the mad, hysterical,
heroined, "don't mean nuthin" nights
of I Corps. GODDAMMIT, I WANNA KNOW WHY

seventeen summers after Vietnam
choppers still coming in, carrying
George Bush, heading for a landing
on his lawn at Kennebunkport, why

seventeen summers after Vietnam
the cast of characters, hardly changed
tomorrow, a photo op for the press
still the same rich white guys, on a lawn.

Mary Pat O'Connor
1990

DREAM OF PEACE

I heard of peace
In the newspaper
I heard of peace
From our leaders' lips

I innocently listened to these words
And cherished the dream of peace
Hoping for the war to end
So that you may give up arms

I heard news from the battlefield
That you've died in combat
Alas! My innocent dream
Was just an agony

Ever since I was born
Ever since I began to understand
I've just witnessed killings
And only blood and bones

Since I knew how to listen
Since I knew how to speak
I've just heard of lies
And of broken promises

Since I began to know how to love
And how to miss my darling
You told me just to wait
But you didn't return

Oh, my innocent dream!
Oh, my dream of peace!
Built up among brutality
And died before its fulfillment

Oh, my tiny heart!
Like a sweet-smelling piece of paper
But an inky spot
Has spoiled everything

I know how to hold a grudge
I understand that life is treacherous
While the front page features peace
The fourth page abounds in obituaries!

I'm no more eager
To believe in what is on other's lips
I begin to be cautious
Just to realize you're gone

Oh, my dream of peace
For which you paid with your own life
And I paid for it with hatred
In all my lonely existence.

Tran Mong Tu
1969
translated by Vann Phan

IT'S TOO EASY

It's too easy to say
What about the just wars?

There are thousands of people
who will be happy to give you
the justification you want.
Just don't ask me to.
I know what war is.
And I will not forget.

Lynda Van Devanter Buckley
1990

CAMOUFLAGE

The green fatigues seem to be everywhere.
Half watching the evening news
I notice,
every story seems to contain men
and even
an occasional woman
In green fatigues or camouflage,
jungle garb
designed for war.
And then, I remember
the children.
The children,
I've seen them so often
at the malls and in the halls
and most recently
at the Wall.
In their green fatigues and camouflage shorts
with matching shirts and hats and socks.
And I think,
I wore green fatigues once.
Bloused over boots and hats and badges
a uniform of war
soiled by blood and mud
and dirt and death.
Unable to be washed clean of
the lingering reminders,
one piece remains
hanging in my closet
near the back.
I can no longer don it
and parade
Nor can I discard it.

So it remains in my closet,
near the back
for me a last reminder
of the devastation
encountered by a youthful mind
who now shuns
thoughts of war
and dreams of peace;
haunted
by the children
playing innocently and walking
by the Wall.
The irony of my vision
stated by tears
for the young men and women
whose last statement
is engraved
in brilliant black granite reflecting
the children
walking by in camouflage sunsuits
smiling.
Unknowingly and unaware
little boys and girls
playing.
While I shudder
at thoughts
of lessons left unlearned.

Joan A. Furey
1984

ARMISTICE DAY

The marching soldiers in parade inspire.
Their uniforms still stir some pride.

But the time that stirs my heart the most
is the two minutes of utter silence
Meant to honor the dead.
Truly peace.

For that's the only time I really leave the "war."
To be with the honored few.

For after the "Vietnam Conflict"
The only really honored were the dead . . .
with silence.

Norma J. Griffiths
1982

KNOWING

*("Recent research indicates Dioxin
is the most potent toxin ever studied."—
news report, September 1987)*

I watched the helicopters
flying slowly north and south
along the DaNang river valley,
trailing a grey mist
which scattered the sun
in murky rainbows.
I never wondered if I knew
all I ought to know
about what they were doing.

I knew that it was called
defoliation,
that the spray would destroy
the hiding places of snipers
and ambushing guerrillas.
I did not know to ask:
at what price?

Every evening,
the sunset choppers arrived
filled with soldiers burning
from jungle fevers:
malaria, dengue, dysentery.
We took them directly
to the cooling showers,
stripped their wet
dirt encrusted uniforms
as we lowered their temperatures

and prepared them for bed.
I did not ask where they had been,
whether they or the uniforms I held
had been caught in the mist,
whether defoliation
had saved their lives.
I did not know to ask.

I knew part of the price
when nine other women
who had watched the helicopters
and seen the mist
talked of their children:
Jason's heart defects, and
Amy's and Rachel's and Timothy's.
Mary's eye problems.
The multiple operations
to make and repair digestive organs
for John and Kathleen and little John.
How lucky they felt
when one child was born healthy
whole.
How they grieved
about the miscarriages
one, two, three, even seven.
Their pain, their helplessness,
their rage when
Marianne died of leukemia at 2,
and Michelle died of cancer at 2½.
Their fear of what might yet happen.

I knew more
when I watched my parents
celebrate their fortieth
wedding anniversary,
four children, three grandchildren
sitting in the pews.
I knew what I would never know,
what the poisons and my fears
have removed forever from my knowing.
The conceiving, the carrying of a child,
the stretching of my womb, my breasts.
The pain of labor.
The bringing forth from my body a new life.

I choose not to know
if my eggs are
misshapen and withered
as the trees along the river.
If snipers are hidden
in the coils of my DNA.

Marilyn McMahon
1988

TV WARS
First Blood Part II

Beside the ship leaving port
For the hot, dry gulf
The white-haired woman says
    I'm proud of my grandson
    He has to go
    To protect our interest.

Dear lady,
Your interest just left on that ship.

    Lynda Van Devanter Buckley
    1990

MIDDLE EAST MONTAGE

Steamy summer sunup
Wearily I sip my morning coffee and
Watch the early news.
A C-130 unloads in the background
The line of soldiers marching across the screen
Wears desert sand camouflage instead of jungle green.
And they're
       still
           just
               kids.

Bryant interviews
Two fresh, young nurses in fatigues.
"We're here to do our part—committed to our country's
   goals."
"We're highly trained and skilled—prepared for anything."
"We've worked civilian ER's, so we've seen it all."
A chill runs through me
My God, they
       have
           no
             idea.

Lynda Van Devanter Buckley
1990

VII
DREAMS

Woven through the dark, bloody tapestry of that year is one golden thread of memory. A small group of us who worked the night shift, sat together at the dawns, reading aloud from ee cummings. Those cherished moments engendered in each of us a new level of compassion and understanding, and helped us to discover the true meaning of duty, honor and country. It was not commitment to a misguided cause, but rather a deep and personal commitment to universal brotherhood and Love. etcetera etcetera etcetera

> **Joan A. Furey** and
> **Lynda Van Devanter Buckley**
> *1969–1990*

PEACE

A single strand
of black velvet
worn to mourn
a world at war
a quiet statement
I am compelled to make.

I find it easier now
to whisper my outrage
rather than screaming
or yelling and stomping my feet
at the insanity
of repetitious attempts
to justify the deaths of so many
in the name of peace and freedom.

Besides,
people seem to pay more
attention to whispers
as if they might miss
some important secret that
will somehow make a difference.

So, if you stop and ask me
about this ribbon that I wear
come very close
and hear my words
that silently spell Peace.

Joan A. Furey
1982

THE STATUE

I envision a statue
of a woman,
a young woman,
standing by the side of a green canvas litter.

Lying on the litter
is a man
a young man, badly wounded
her right hand is clutching his.

Though I recall our hands were too busy to do that,
our hearts did it
till they became numb.

I can look into her eyes
and see the pain and fatigue.
It only shows there.

I guess when heroes dream of statues,
they dream of men with guns.

I dream of a woman
with only her heart, hands and mind
her "weapons"
to deal with the world of carnage.

Norma J. Griffiths
1982

CORAL BAY

Tonight I spoke
  of reason and purpose
    of issues and answers
      of lessons to live and lessons to learn
I thought of chance
  of encounters unexpected
    of people passing
      of moving by
Tonight, in the still harbor
  of a Caribbean cove
    in a ramshackle bar
      and restaurant and store
I chanced upon
  a man named Tom
    who walked with aid
      of rubber wheels
Who talked of sea
  and air and breeze
    of looking forward
      far and fast
Who left behind
  the thoughts of war
    of life, of death
      of struggles to survive
The loss of legs
  in distant land
    left in the jungles
      of Vietnam
A life lay shattered
  for many months
    fucked up, drugged up
      in stoned despair

— 197 —

Who arose
    to survive
        to renew
            alive
Then learned to sail
    to build to grow
        to pioneer in
            this rugged land
With aid of heart
    of soul of mind
        who looks to the dawn
            of each new day
To the seas
    to the breeze
        to the sail
            away

Joan A. Furey
1983

INITIATED IN AGONY

Initiated in agony by insensate physiology,
today I join my smiling foremothers in secret sorority
as I hold my firstborn son in my arms.
The air echoes with mysteries whispered about
by ageless unseen women bound and covered
gathered at the wells and marketplaces and courtyards,
sandaled footsteps sibilant on stone
stirring dust as they chatter of intimate concerns,
of pain and peril, virgin giggles of wonder and delight,
novices in simple and everyday miracles.

Five pounds of promise and possibility
I cradle him very, very close.
Exhaustion invites idle musings
of his future triumphs and delights,
mighty challenges and conquerings,
amid the humble routine dailiness of his mother's boundless
    love.
Today I am a lifegiver, a deliverer of futures and dreams.
All the things that love can wish, I wish for him, of him,
and in his name.

Womanly, motherly emotions I weave
as tightly around my heart as I possibly can
a garment of mail to guard against intimations of disaster
of knowings I would rather not face.
Sarah, when you laughed, was there no tint of tragedy
in the future-pictures of your love's imaginings?
Hannah, could you dream your womb's longing
would be so cruelly fulfilled?
Mary, how did you bear to bear the child
whose destruction was foretold?

I look at this tiny face and see
shadows of boy-warriors' suffering,
bodies torn beyond my powers of solace
answering the voices of the mighty
to offer themselves for the honor of cowards.
If I should bear a dozen sons
I shall never understand:
Why did you not warn me, my mothers,
Why did you not speak of this,
that mothers would suffer such unbearable love
that men would inflict such a terrible price?

Dana Shuster
1974

THE PEACE TO END ALL WARS

Let us think no more
of the "war to end all wars"

for only in complete destruction of all
would that be possible.

So let us think
of the Peace to end all wars
and perhaps
finally, working with the right tool
we can create the goal.

Norma J. Griffiths
1982

THE MOON IS A NUISANCE

The moon is a nuisance.
It rises from behind the hogback ridge
spilling light down the snowy slope.
Like an assailant, moonlight slips
into the temporary darkroom in my kitchen.
It falls prey upon the black and white
photograph emerging in developer
turning the image grey.

I discard the print
shift my chemicals away from the window
expose another piece of paper
slide it into developer.
I look closely at the image
see myself perched
on a palm trunk bridge
in Viet Nam.

The Vietnamese woman beside me looks planted
her toes spread like fingers
gripping the trunk.
Second Treasure
who once fought U.S. soldiers
looks pleased
standing by an American.

The photo washes and I stare
out my kitchen window.
A silver fox lopes through the moonlight.
I imagine taking Second Treasure into
this bitter cold.
Then, it would be her turn to feel tentative.

I picture her donning layers of wool.
For the first time she puts on shoes.
Every step into the wintry moonlight brings
cautious wonder that the world can turn
white.

In the barn, Second Treasure removes a mitten
to test Foxy Cow's winter fur.
Icicles on Foxy's whiskers shatter
into Second Treasure's palm.
"And look at you," she says, touching
the hair around my cap.
"Twenty years older!"
I laugh, knowing breath has frosted
my hair to silver.

The Ohio moon that could light our way to the barn
is a nuisance
penetrating this kitchen darkroom. At midnight,
it has intensity like the midday sun
at this same moment
dappling a palm trunk bridge
in Viet Nam.

The moonlight grazes
the newly washed photograph—
two women
one tentative, the other assured.
The moon's glow tempers
their black and white
differences.

Lady Borton
1990

FOR MOLLY

What did you do in the war, Mommy?
Hazel eyes shining brightly
Pony tails bobbing softly
One pierced earring and an orange juice mustache.

Where did that man's arm go, Mommy?
Plastic slinky bouncing wildly
Tie dye T-shirt hanging loosely
Looks at me so earnestly I have to touch her.

I wrote a story about a war Mommy.
Where nobody got guns or dead
This one was a good war
Don't you know?

Why do you have tears now, Mommy?
Little girl with dreams so peaceful
Alphabets and clowns and people
I don't want you growing up too soon.

Lynda Van Devanter Buckley
1990

MAKING FRIENDS

Twenty years since my life was changed
Twenty years making a friend of death
Knowing it
Respecting it
Wishing for it at times
Fighting with it as friends sometimes do.

But the nightmares of war have faded as I've healed
My dreams are now of peace
Peace of mind
Peace of heart
Hoping for Peace on earth
It's time I made a friend of Life.

Lynda Van Devanter Buckley
1990

GLOSSARY

AFVN: Armed Forces Vietnam Network, Radio and TV.

Ao Dais: Traditional Vietnamese women's dresses, long, airy and flowing.

APC: Armed Personnel Carrier.

A-K Amp: Above Knee Amputation.

Big PX: The Land of the Big PX—i.e. back in the U.S.

Bouncing Betty: Land mine that shoots an explosive charge up to waist level before detonating.

C-130: Large U.S. Air Force transport and cargo plane.

Cobra: U.S. Army attack helicopter.

Crispy Critters: Slang for burned patients.

Defoliant: Toxic chemical sprayed over heavy vegetation to clear it. Used by the U.S. in Vietnam to deny cover and food to the enemy.

Dengue: Acute disease characterized by high fevers.

DEROS: Date of Expected Return from Overseas Station.

ER: Emergency Room.

Evaced: Evacuated to the next level of care.

Geckoes: Small lizards native to tropical areas.

Ginkos: A broad-leafed tree native to Asia.

Gook: Unfortunate, derogatory term for the Vietnamese people.

Gork: Slang expression for a patient who is severely neurologically impaired and comatose.

GRU: Graves Registration Unit.

Grunts: Infantry soldiers.

Hootch: Living quarters.

ICU: Intensive Care Unit.

Incoming: Rockets or mortars fired by the enemy at our troops.

Jarhead: Slang term for a Marine.

JP-4: Jet fuel.

Lactated Ringers: Intravenous solution used as a blood volume expander.

Mix-n-Match: Mass casualty situation in which numerous patients have sustained multiple amputations.

Montagnards: Primitive people who live in Vietnam's Central Highlands.

OR: Operating Room.

P-52s: Small Air Force planes.

Post-Op: Post Operative ward.

R & E: Receiving and Emergency, the triage area.

Short: Having only a little amount of time left to serve in Vietnam.

The World: The United States of America—home.

Train Wrecks: Many casualties with multiple traumatic injuries.

Triage: Sorting casualties into three categories: 1: Immediate care required, 2: Can wait, 3: Expectant—probably will not live, give only comfort care.

White Phosphorous Mine: Incendiary explosive device containing phosphorous, which causes chemical burns.

BIBLIOGRAPHY

Adams, Lily Lee, in *Connections*, Newsletter of the William Joiner Center for the Study of War and Social Consequences, University of Massachusetts at Boston, June, 1990.

Allen, Elizabeth, in *China Beach*, "The Veterans," Warner Bros. TV, 1990.

Borton, Lady, *Sensing the Enemy*, Dial Press, Doubleday, New York, 1984.

Dusty, in *Shrapnel in the Heart*, edited by Laura Palmer, Random House, New York, 1987.

Emerson, Gloria, *Winners and Losers—Battles, Retreats, Gains, Losses and Ruins from a Long War*, Random House, New York, 1972.

Farmborough, Florence, *Nurse at the Russian Front: A Diary 1914–1918*, Constable and Co., London, 1974.

Griffiths, Norma J., in *Connections*, Ibid.

Harrod, Bernadette, in *Connections*, Ibid.

Liem, Gracie, in *In the Combat Zone*, edited by Kathryn Marshall, Little, Brown & Co., Boston, 1987.

McMahon, Marilyn, in *Works in Progress I* and *Works in Progress II*, Seattle, 1988 and 1990.

Nerli, Maureen, in *A Piece of My Heart,* edited by Keith Walker, Presidio Press, Novato, CA., 1985.

Palmer, Laura, in *Shrapnel in the Heart,* Random House, New York, 1987.

Redmond, Juanita, *I Served on Bataan,* J.B. Lippincott, Philadelphia, 1943.

Smith, Gayle, in *Everything We Had,* edited by Albert Santoli, Random House, New York, 1981.

Trotter, Bobbie, in *Connections,* Ibid.

Woodham-Smith, Cecil, *Florence Nightingale 1820–1910,* McGraw-Hill, New York, 1951.

ABOUT THE POETS

Lily Lee Adams served in Vietnam with the Army Nurse Corps at the 12th Evacuation Hospital in Cu Chi from 1969 to 1970.

Lady Borton worked with the American Friends Service Committee in Quang Ngai from 1969 to 1971. She returned to Southeast Asia in 1980 to work with Vietnamese boat people on the Malaysian island of Pulau Bidong, and again in 1990 to work in Vietnam.

Mary Lu Ostergren Brunner served as an Operating Room nurse in Vietnam with the Army Nurse Corps at the 71st Evacuation Hospital in Pleiku from 1968 to 1969.

Joan Arrington Craigwell served as an Air Force Nurse in Cam Rahn Bay in 1967 and 1968. She worked in a triage unit, the 26th Casualty Staging Unit and as a flight nurse.

Judith Drake was a member of the 1965 international company of "Hello Dolly." The production played in Saigon, and at many airbases in Vietnam.

Dusty served with the Army Nurse Corps in the Iron Triangle area of Vietnam. She worked in critical care units.

Diane Carlson Evans served with the Army Nurse Corps in 1968 and 1969 at the 36th Evacuation Hospital in Vung Tau and the 71st Evacuation Hospital in Pleiku.

Penni Evans served with the American Red Cross in 1970 and 1971. She was stationed in Cam Rahn Bay, Cu Chi and Quang Tri, and with II Field Force.

Margaret Flatt served in Vung Tau with the Army Nurse Corps at the 36th Evacuation Hospital from 1967 to 1968.

Joan A. Furey served with the Army Nurse Corps in Pleiku at the 71st Evacuation Hospital from 1969 to 1970. She worked in the Post-Op/Intensive Care Unit as an Army Nurse.

Mary Beyers Garrison served with the Army Nurse Corps at the 24th Evacuation Hospital in Long Binh in 1968 and 1969.

Sharon Grant served with the Army Nurse Corps from 1970 to 1971 at the 67th Evacuation Hospital in Qui Nhon and at the 71st Evacuation Hospital in Pleiku. She was an OR Nurse.

Norma J. Griffiths served with the Army Nurse Corps in 1969 and 1970 at the 67th Evacuation Hospital in Qui Nhon as an Emergency Room/Triage Nurse.

Ha Phuong was born and raised near Cu Chi in Vietnam. During the war she spent time living in the tunnels of Cu Chi.

Bernadette Harrod served in the Army Nurse Corps at the 22nd Surgical Hospital at Phu Bai in 1968 and 1969. She was an OR Nurse.

Kathleen Harty served with the Army Nurse Corps at the 36th

Evacuation Hospital at Vung Tau in 1968 and 1969. She worked in ER and ICU.

Huong Tram was born and raised in Vietnam. She is a well known Vietnamese poet.

Diane C. Jaeger served with the Army Nurse Corps at the 24th Evacuation Hospital in Long Binh. She worked in the Neurosurgical ICU.

Penny Kettlewell served two tours of duty with the Army Nurse Corps in Vietnam. In 1967 and 1968, she was stationed at the 67th Evacuation Hospital in Qui Nhon, and in 1970 and 1971 she served at the 24th Evacuation Hospital in Long Binh.

Joyce A. Merrill served in the Air Force Nurse Corps in Cam Rahn Bay in 1969 and 1970. She worked on the Critical Care Unit.

Marilyn McMahon served in the Navy Nurse Corps at Da Nang Naval Hospital in 1969 and 1970.

Sara J. McVicker served in the Army Nurse Corps at the 71st Evacuation Hospital in 1969 and 1970.

Minh Duc Hoai Trinh was born in Vietnam, and raised in France. She returned to become a renowned writer and journalist in Saigon. She now lives in the United States.

Nguyen Ngoc Xuan was born in Cholon, Vietnam. During the 1968 Tet offensive, she was wounded by shrapnel, and later burned during a bombing attack on her village. She now lives in the United States.

Mary Pat O'Connor served as a Red Cross Volunteer at the Camp Kue Army Hospital in Okinawa in 1968 and 1969.

Grace Paley was in Vietnam in 1969 as a member of a delegation of anti-war activists whose purpose was to bring home American POWs. She traveled North Vietnam from Hanoi to the 17th parallel.

Helen DeCrane Roth served with the Navy Nurse Corps in Vietnam in 1968 and 1969. She worked in the Operating Room on the USS Sanctuary, one of two Navy Hospital Ships which saw duty in Vietnam.

Winifred Cochrane Schramm served with the Army Nurse Corps during World War II in North Africa and Italy. She was assigned to the surgical teams at the 56th Evacuation Hospital and the 105th Station Hospital, and served at Anzio during the beachhead invasion.

Linda Spoonster Schwartz served with the U.S. Air Force at the USAF Hospital in Tachikawa, Japan from 1968 to 1971.

Dana Shuster served in the Army Nurse Corps in Vietnam for two tours of duty from 1966 to 1968. She worked in the OR, ER and ICU.

Joan Parrot Skiba served in the Army Nurse Corps in Vietnam in 1969 and 1979. She worked in ER at the 18th Surgical Hospital in Camp Evans and the 71st Evacuation Hospital in Pleiku.

Lou McCurdy Sorrin served with the Army Nurse Corps at the 12th Evacuation Hospital in Cu Chi and the 67th Evacuation Hospital in Qui Nhon in 1968 and 1969. She worked in the ICU.

Emily Strange served with the American Red Cross in Vietnam at the 9th Infantry Division in Dong Tam.

Tran Mong Tu was born in Ha Dong, Vietnam. During the war she worked for the Associated Press in Saigon. She is a well-known poet in the Vietnamese community. She now lives in the United States.

Kathleen Trew served with the Army Nurse Corps at the 93rd Evacuation Hospital in Long Binh in 1969 and 1970.

Bobbie Trotter served with the American Red Cross in Vietnam where she traveled to firebases, hospitals, advisory camps and clinics.

Mary O'Brien Tyrrell served in 1967 and 1968 with the Navy Nurse Corps as head nurse of the D2 Air Evac Ward at the US Naval Hospital on Guam.

Lynda Van Devanter served with the Army Nurse Corps as an OR nurse in 1969 and 1970. She was stationed at the 71st Evacuation Hospital in Pleiku and the 67th Evacuation Hospital in Qui Nhon.

Janet Krouse Wyatt served with the Army Nurse Corps as an ICU and ER nurse in 1969. She was stationed at the 71st Evacuation Hospital in Pleiku.

Xuan Quynh was born and raised in Vietnam. Until her death in the early 1980s, she was the most famous woman poet in Vietnam. She and her infant son lived in the tunnels for some time during the war. She was killed in a car accident along with her husband and her then 12-year-old son.